# Walking Healed

# Walking Healed

## A Journey of Forgiveness, Grace, and Hope

Shelley Wilburn

# Walking Healed

Copyright © 2015 Shelley Wilburn
Second edition, Copyright © 2016 Shelley Wilburn

All rights reserved. No part of this publication may be reproduced, stored in a retrieval system, or transmitted in any form or by any means, electronic, mechanical, photocopying, recording, or otherwise without the prior written permission of the author. Reviewers may quote briefly for review purposes.

All Scripture quotations, unless otherwise indicated, are taken from the *Holy Bible, New International Version*®. *NIV*®. Copyright © 1973, 1978, 1984 by International Bible Society. Used by permission of Zondervan. All rights reserved.

Scripture quotations are taken from the *Holy Bible*, New Living Translation (NLT), copyright ©1996. Used by permission of Tyndale House Publishers, Inc. Carol Stream, IL USA. All rights reserved.

Scripture quotations marked "NKJV" are taken from the New King James version. Copyright ©1982. Used by Thomas Nelson Inc. Used by permission. All rights reserved.

Scripture quotations marked HCSB are taken from the Holman Christian Standard Bible®, Copyright © 1999, 2000, 2002, 2003, 2009 by Holman Bible Publishers. Used by permission. Holman Christian Standard Bible®, Holman CSB®, and HCSB® are federally registered trademarks of Holman Bible Publishers.

All Scripture quotations, unless otherwise indicated, are taken from the *Amplified Bible*, Old Testament. Copyright © 1965 1987 by the Zondervan Corporation. Used by permission. All rights reserved.

All Scripture quotations, unless otherwise indicated, are taken from the *Amplified Bible*, New Testament. Copyright © 1954, 1958, 1987 by the Lockman Foundation. Used by permission.

Cover art on second edition by Rodney Schroeter
Edited by Lisa J Lickel
Swirl design image courtesy of clickr.com

## Mismatched Socks Productions
Print - ISBN 978-0-9864311-0-4
e-Book - ISBN 978-0-9864311-1-1
Library of Congress Control Number: 2015902208

Published in the United States of America

**Mismatched Socks Productions**

# Table of Contents

My Sincerest Thanks ................................................................. 8
Introduction ............................................................................... 9
My Journey to Forgiveness ..................................................... 12
Breaking the Chains ................................................................ 14
Mending Fences ....................................................................... 17
Offense and Defense ................................................................ 21
Revelation to Revolution ......................................................... 25
Get Rid of Your "BUT!" ......................................................... 29
God Can Still Use You ............................................................ 32
Detour on the Road Trip ......................................................... 34
Sticks and Stones ..................................................................... 37
Stop Listening to Lies .............................................................. 40
Deflating Balloons ................................................................... 43
Past Is Past ............................................................................... 46
Take Off Your Mask ................................................................ 49
Finding Your Treasure ............................................................ 51
Do It Afraid .............................................................................. 54
Setting Boundaries .................................................................. 57
Shields Up! ............................................................................... 60
Mass Communicating .............................................................. 62
Healing Rain ............................................................................ 65
Freedom ................................................................................... 68
Make Up Your Mind ................................................................ 71
Moving Forward ...................................................................... 74

| | |
|---|---|
| Wisdom In Reconciling | 77 |
| When Friendships Fail | 80 |
| Beauty for Ashes | 83 |
| Water on the Rocks | 87 |
| Overcoming Fear | 89 |
| Label Makers | 91 |
| Learning to Let Go | 93 |
| No One Like You | 95 |
| Cracked Pots | 97 |
| Don't Miss the Point | 99 |
| From Duh to Aha! | 102 |
| Grace Who? | 104 |
| Do Yourself A Favor | 106 |
| Got Junk in Your Trunk? | 109 |
| Comfort Training | 111 |
| Trust Issues | 113 |
| Stepping Onto the | 117 |
| Perfectly, Powerfully, and Permanently | 120 |
| Setbacks, Struggles, and Stress | 123 |
| Moving On! | 128 |
| Can't Keep Me Down! | 131 |
| Where Do I Fit In?! | 133 |
| Short-Circuited | 135 |
| My Chains Are Gone! | 137 |
| You Are On Purpose | 140 |
| Answer the Phone | 142 |
| Ch-Ch-Ch-Changes | 145 |

| | |
|---|---|
| Leave Your Light On | 148 |
| Put Your Foot Down | 151 |
| I Am a Lazarus | 155 |
| A Year In My Life | 158 |
| Stop People Pleasing | 161 |
| Because I Love You | 164 |
| Don't Back Up | 168 |
| Grab a Hold | 171 |
| Rose-Colored Glasses | 174 |
| Zombies…the | 177 |
| What Are You Doing Here? | 181 |
| Reckless | 184 |
| Unlocking Your Door | 188 |
| God's Favor…is NOW! | 191 |
| Far Out! | 194 |
| Rescuing People | 196 |
| Discovering My More | 200 |
| Snakes in the Garden | 203 |
| Changing Your Life | 205 |
| Where Do I Go From Here? | 209 |
| Parting Words | 215 |
| About the Author | 217 |
| Appendix A | 219 |
| Appendix B | 222 |
| Notes | 224 |

# My Sincerest Thanks

So many people come to mind when thinking about who to thank. I probably can't name all of them, but I'm going to give it a shot anyway.

First of all, I want to thank Jesus. Because, without You I wouldn't be where I am right now. What the devil meant for harm, You turned it around and made it good. You literally worked all things together for good, and You're always working things toward the better, giving me double back of what was taken from me. So, thank You.

To my wonderful soul mate and best-good-friend-ever-on-this-earth, Don Athen Wilburn. Thank you for seeing *me* all those years ago; for really "seeing" me, past all the junk and into my soul. Only God could give you that vision. Thank you for standing by me and with me, and for never giving up on me. Your support and your love mean more than you'll ever know. You truly are "such a good husband."

To Rachel and Jake, Brett and Katie, and Logan and Rhiannon. You've all been my life and entertainment through the years. Now that you're all grown up, though you're my kids, you're the best friends I could ever ask for. Thanks for keeping me grounded and rooted.

To Radley, Abraham, and Jude; Nonney loves you big! You're all going to be great men of God someday! Do great things for Him, and Nonney will be your biggest cheerleader.

To Patty, Lisa, and Karla, thanks for the support and the encouragement. Without you I wouldn't have a website, a platform, speaking engagements, and been launched into the world of writers. You are my heroes.

And to you, dear reader: Thank you for reading.

# Introduction

I was looking at a wedding picture of my husband and me not long ago. As I looked at myself from thirty-one years ago, I stared at the young girl I used to be. I saw in that girl all of the pent-up hurts, depression, intimidation, and mental and emotional scars that she carried but didn't know what to do with.

As I sat there, I distinctly felt a question skim through my heart, "Would you change any of that?" I immediately knew the answer and, smiling, I replied, "Not for the world!" Why? Because the things that girl went through shaped me into who I am today.

Living with intimidation, oppression, depression, panic, and anxiety takes a toll on a person. We don't often know why we are going through the things we are. We can't explain the feelings we have or why we do the things we do. Many people don't understand depression or the people suffering from it. They also don't understand panic and anxiety attacks. However, these feelings are very real.

For over forty years I suffered bouts of depression, panic, and anxiety. I also dealt with intimidation, oppression, and an eating disorder. I ate everything I could get my hands on because food was my comfort, my "drug of choice." My nerve problems started at the age of six. I was labeled as a nervous child. My home life though consisted of a lot of yelling and arguments between my parents, hence the nerve problems. They didn't end until May 30, 2012, when God literally healed me from the inside out.

It was at this time God opened the floodgates of my gift and love of writing and I began to pour out my story on a blog, a website diary of sorts. I was hoping to get the story out to others who suffered like I did. I hoped that through what I wrote that someone out there would be encouraged, that someone would find hope, that someone would find forgiveness, or even healing.

It has taken me the better part of two years to write my story. I truly believe God has called me to become transparent so that someone out there will read it and realize God wants to heal you, too.

Trust me when I say I had no idea this would happen. I have always loved writing. I have always wanted to write a book. But I really never knew my desire for writing would end up where it is now. I could never channel my writing due to the mental and emotional garbage I lived with most of my life. I just didn't know what to do with it, or how to get rid of it.

Through these pages would you walk along with me as I walk out my healing? You can watch as my life changes with each turn of the page, each story that is documented. This is my journey of two years. It may read like a devotional in some areas. It may read like a diary in others. Through it all, God has been in the very center molding and remaking everything about me.

Each entry has the date it was written. Each deals with something that was placed upon my heart. Whether it's breaking the chains of intimidation and depression, stopping listening to the lies of the enemy, overcoming fear, or

*Walking Healed*

overcoming being wounded, each entry has a story. Each story has a purpose and uplifting Scriptures from the Lord to help you deal with the things you're going through.

This is as transparent as I am. I truly hope that you find solace in the pages of this book. God wants to do a mighty work in you, too. You are not hopeless. You are not forgotten. You are definitely not too far gone. God is the God of many chances. He loves you dearly. He wants to heal you.

I'm not where I want to be. But I'm also definitely not where I used to be. I'm not the same person I was forty years ago. I'm not even the same person I was last week! That's the beauty of the healing hand of the Lord. He is always changing and rearranging you, making you into the person He created you to be. It's a journey; a journey to forgiveness, a journey of grace, a journey of hope. This is a journey to find your purpose, and you do have one!

I do hope that through my story, you can find healing in yours.

It's an exciting time for all of us! Come along with me on the walk through my healing and may you find forgiveness, grace, and hope during our travels, along with your purpose.

I love you, dear friend!

~Sincerely from my heart,

Shelley

Shelley Wilburn

# My Journey to Forgiveness
**June 2, 2012**

This is a journey for me. It's also something I've never done before. I have written blogs before, but they were not what God wanted me to do. Over the last couple of days, beginning Wednesday, May 30th, the Lord has taken me on a journey of healing and forgiveness. He has brought me out of a pit of despair, oppression, depression, confusion, anger, bitterness; years of hurt, scars, fear and mental anguish.

I have been healed of many things that have been pressing me down for years. And the Lord is going to use that to help you get out of your pit, too. Why would I tell my story now rather than later? I believe it's never too early or too late to tell your story.

"And do not be conformed to this world, but be transformed by the renewing of your mind, that you may prove what is that good and acceptable and perfect will of God." ~Romans 12:2 (NKJV)

This is for you, whoever you are. Whether you know it or not, I have been sent to help you because right now, you are being beaten up mentally, emotionally, and spiritually, by other women and maybe some men, too. They may be your family. They may be friends. I don't know. But God does.

Let me tell you what the devil did to me. Then let me

tell you how the Lord delivered me from it. You won't regret it. You may even be healed as you travel this journey with me. We're going to laugh. We're going to cry. And we're going to learn how the Lord can help you. And He will. I promise. He promises.

"The thief does not come except to steal, and to kill, and to destroy. I have come that they may have life, and that they may have it more abundantly." ~John 10:10 (NKJV)

Are you ready? In the following pages there will be little stories from my life that will show you how I was mentally and emotionally abused by several women, family members, friends and others in my life over the years; some whom I love. You will learn what God wants to say to you through this journey. As we go along, you will see how God placed many different people in my life to help guide me in the direction that he needed me to go in order to get me to the place I am now. My journey can be your journey. I found the way out of depression, intimidation, and the things pressing in on me that controlled me for so long. And I'm here to show you the way out, too. Let's journey together.

Shelley Wilburn

# Breaking the Chains
**June 4**

Oppressed. That was me. For nearly forty-seven years. I lived my life always trying to please others. Always seeking the approval of others. And always falling short. I was always weighed, measured, and found wanting by the very people who should have loved me unconditionally. Oh they loved me. But if I messed up, if I did something they didn't like, I heard about it continually.

I would say I was sorry, always wondering what I did to make them mad. They would "forgive" me, yet come back with a barrage of faults of mine, beginning with "But you..." When I would begin to cry, I would hear, "Dry it up! You brought this on yourself!" I'm still trying to figure out what I did. But you know what? It does not matter now.

When I accepted Jesus into my life, I had no earthly idea that I didn't have to perform for Him to get Him to love me. I had no idea that He would never bring up my past mistakes (and let me tell you, I have made many). I had no idea that He loved me unconditionally. All I had to do was trust Him. But I didn't know how. For twenty-nine years, I ran around trying to figure out this God, this Jesus, whom everyone around me seems to know in an intimately spiritual way. What was I missing? Did I even have Him in my heart at all? I did have Him in my heart, but I'd never really got to know Him intimately; never really given Him total control of my life. I mean, everyone else had control of it; wouldn't God just do me the same way? Absolutely not!

You see, I have been oppressed for most of my life. I have been beat down and intimidated by many women in my life. Many of them family members. Many of them other people. People who think they know what I should be doing. People who think they know me. Many people would love to tell you "what she's really like."

Let me tell you, they don't know. They never have. No one has ever seen the real Shelley. Not my parents, not my siblings, not my kids, not my extended family, no one. Not until now. And it's going to take a while for all of her to surface even now, but I'm working on it.

I'm not laying blame on anyone, I'm not accusing anyone. I'm just stating facts. What I am saying is that being a people pleaser has not got me anywhere in life. In doing so, I have let people walk all over me, dictating which direction I go and what I do. If someone didn't like what I was doing, I quit it. It didn't matter what it was, I quit. When I would hear things like, "What do you want to do *that* for?" I would literally feel the weight crushing my chest, pressing in, almost suffocating me. When I would stop doing anything for myself, those accusations would stop. It never occurred to me that I was being oppressed and controlled.

Let me tell you what the devil did to me. He used my family members, my friends, people I went to church with, and many others to control me and to keep me from a ministry that the Lord was calling me into. And I let them. But, when the Spirit of the Lord came upon me that night in church, I had no idea that that's what if felt like. That's what He felt like! It was like breaking the chains of bondage that had held me captive for almost forty-seven years of my life the crushing weight was lifted. I could breathe. No more panic. No more anxiety. Just peace, happiness, laughter, song, and a whole barrage of other things I can't explain other than to say, that was God! I literally felt as if the Lord was saying to me, "You've done this long enough. I need you for a ministry, and you need to follow Me."

"The Spirit of the Lord [is] upon Me, because He has anointed Me to announce release to the captives...to send forth as delivered those who are oppressed..." ~Luke 4:18 (Amplified Bible)

I had been writing notes for a book about forgiveness in a journal for nearly four months. I knew I was going to go on a journey to find forgiveness in my heart for those who have oppressed me throughout the years. But I didn't know how I was going to get there. I love them. I wanted to forgive them. When the Holy Spirit washed over me that Wednesday night and I collapsed in the floor, I found that forgiveness. I also found my ministry and the rest of the notes for the book. I went down an oppressed, depressed, unhappy woman. I got up a liberated, free, changed one.

My story isn't finished yet...it's only beginning. There are going to be trials. There are going to be confrontations. Many of those who have oppressed me for years are going to continue to try to intimidate me and keep me down. But one thing they don't realize is that they can't do it to me again.

If what you have just read sounds like you, I want you to know something. You don't have to live like I did. No matter what anyone else tells you, there is a God who loves you for you. He adores you! Come to Him and let Him break the chains of your bondage, too.

# Mending Fences
**June 6**

We all have broken fences. Those make us very unhappy. Wouldn't we all love to have happiness all the time? We don't though. But we could have an abundance. In my journey to forgiveness, it's not just about asking the Lord to forgive me. I already have that. But it's a journey for me to forgive others. Whether they choose to forgive me is upon them. I can't make them forgive me. Many of them don't want to. Many of them never will. They would rather lay the blame with me and leave it there. And I can't worry about that, because I have asked the Lord to forgive me. I also know who I can go to and ask them to forgive, and the ones whom I can't go to. To do that would open up another venue for them to attack me once again, trying to bully and control me. Now don't think for one minute that I haven't tried. I have. You may wonder, "Now Shelley, you need to keep trying..." It's not about that. But the Lord has placed it upon me to write this and there is someone out there going through the same things that I have gone through. I'm here to tell you what God's Word says about that so that you too, can mend your fences and find happiness within. You may think you're happy, but somewhere deep inside we all have a longing to be able to have peace with everyone, whether it's doable or not.

"You make known to me the path of life; you will fill me

with joy in your presence, with eternal pleasures at your right hand." ~Psalm 16:11 (NIV)

There are people in your life who have caused division. I have them in mine. And I love most of those people, but here's where it gets tricky. Even though I love those people, I can't be around them. Because these are the people who pick at me, disguising it as joking and not meaning anything by it and who like to try to get a rise out of me and make me stumble. When I do stumble, they laugh at me and say, "Well, I thought you were supposed to be a goody-two-shoes Christian?" Christian yes, goody-two-shoes, no.

"Now I urge you, brethren, note those who cause divisions and offenses, contrary to the doctrine which you learned, and avoid them. For those who are such do not serve our Lord Jesus Christ, but their own belly, and by smooth words and flattering speech deceive the hearts of the simple." ~Romans 16:17-18 (NKJV)

One day I spent the morning on the phone with someone I adored when I was growing up. We had a wedge driven between us by family members we both loved dearly and who are no longer with us. We had been played against one another, being compared to each other and always coming up lacking or being told one was not as good as the other. Comparison brought jealousy. Neither felt we were good enough. It filtered down to our children being rivaled; who had the best grades, who had more talent, etc. For several years we didn't speak to each other because we each thought the other had a problem, but neither of us couldn't figure out what we had done to each other to deserve being treated with years of non-communication, years of wondering why, years of asking ourselves, "What did I do?" Each was willing to let the other go because we had to move on with our own lives. However, because one of us made the move to reach out, we were now on speaking terms, but those questions still remained. Why? What had I done to cause the rift? God directed the conversation though and many truths came out and both of us were surprised and healed.

"Moreover, if your brother sins against you, go and tell him his fault between you and him alone. If he hears you, you have gained your brother." ~Matthew 18:15 (NKJV)

There will be times when you know without a shadow of a doubt that the person who has hurt you will not receive what you have to say. This person may take your confrontation and use it against you. For example, when trying to bring the way they hurt you to the surface and talk it through, they may twist your words and throw them back at you, making you the guilty person. They may say that it was actually you who said them or you who did this to them. In reality, none of this is true, but you've been victimized once again. This is a tragic loss because that person is close minded, and hard-hearted. There is something inside them that has turned cold. You must then turn them over to the Lord and let Him deal with them. There is not one thing you can do to make things right with that person. The hardest thing for me was to pray for those in my life who are that way. Always before though, I wanted to hurt them as much as they hurt me. But I had to forgive. I had to get to that point. Having others pray for me is what helped break through the years of hurt and oppression. God released me of it. I'm telling you today that the devil will keep you down in any way he can to keep you from mending fences, whether it's with others or within yourself, or with the Lord.

"Be serious! Be alert! Your adversary the Devil is prowling around like a roaring lion, looking for anyone he can devour. Resist him and be firm in the faith, knowing that the same sufferings are being experienced by your fellow believers throughout the world." ~1 Peter 5:8-9 (HCSB)

You are not alone. That's one reason why I'm writing this. I've been there. I will repeat this many, many times: God healed me of a lifetime of oppression, intimidation, and hurts. I've come out of the pit, out of the fog, and it's a new day. Those who have un-forgiveness in their hearts will not understand that, but those of you seeking to find what I did will find it. Believe it. Receive it. Mend your fences and be healed.

# Offense and Defense
**June 7**

For as long as I can remember, any time anyone questioned something I said or did, I became defensive. It didn't matter what it was. If I was questioned, I immediately got defensive. Not only that, but after the confrontation I would sit and analyze what had just happened. I would run through the scenario again and again...and again, imagining what I could have said or done differently.

"When she said this, I should have said that," I would tell myself. Then I would go through the scene another time, imagining it differently. I would do this until I became so mad and offended that I couldn't think at all. I was in a constant state of turmoil, stress, tension and angst. But I covered it and hid it behind Scripture and my pitiful attempts at prayer. I would sit down to do my prayer journal and begin by asking God to watch over this one and that one, and then I would ask Him to forgive me for the things I say and do. Before long, I had no idea where I was going with the prayer. I just had mindless wandering. I wanted to pray for those who had offended me, but I didn't know what exactly I should pray for. I would read about forgiveness in the Bible, but I didn't know how to forgive others as Christ had forgiven me.

"And forgive us our debts, as we forgive our debtors."

Shelley Wilburn

~Matthew 6:12 (NKJV)

This is how the enemy uses people to cause you to take your eyes off of Christ. Someone will say something to you, you become defensive, then you become offended. I talked earlier about breaking the chains. Once those chains are broken, we need to get rid of them so that the remaining pieces don't collect to form another way to keep us in bondage (slavery). And they will! The enemy will use what's left to remind you of past hurts. He will bring up old stuff in your mind to remind you of how you handled things before the Lord broke your chains of slavery. So don't get defensive, and definitely don't get offended.

"Christ has liberated us to be free. Stand firm then and don't submit again to a yoke of slavery." ~Galatians 5:1 (HCSB)

How do you do that? Get into God's Word. Read. Pray. First Thessalonians 5:17 says to "pray without ceasing." But how do we pray without stopping? It's very simple. I used to get so confused when trying to figure out how to continually pray. My worst time with having negative, oppressive thoughts pop into my head are when I'm doing dishes, laundry, or when I lay down in bed at night. Those are the times when little things pop in there. I'm not even going to write them because once they start it's like a snowball effect and they keep growing and growing. It's best to stay away from them and not make them a rerun in your head. So what I'm going to tell you instead is, this is when you have to put a stop to it. If you have to, say out loud, "No!"

"Resist the devil and he will flee from you." ~James 4:7b (NKJV)

The enemy only has the power that you give to him. So don't give it to him. We have been beaten down so much that we think God can't fix our problem, or that He doesn't care, or that our problems are too many and God can't take care of all of them at once. That is a lie. You and I have more power in the tips of our little finger than the devil does in his whole body. You do not have to be oppressed anymore. You do not have to listen to the lies the enemy tells you. When you begin to have those crippling thoughts, say out loud, No! Shake your head no. Start calling out to God. This is praying without ceasing. This is what I mean by it. Every time the negativity starts, you start talking to God. Whether you have to speak out loud or pray in your thoughts, God can hear you no matter what. When my mind was so full of junk that I couldn't concentrate on praying silently, I prayed out loud. I would whisper, or talk normally, or sometimes even cry out with a loud voice. But I have to stand up for myself both in the flesh and in the spirit. I have to take back my life and hand it over to God. He can do so much more with it than I can.

"Therefore take up the whole armor of God that you may be able to withstand in the evil day, and having done all, to stand." ~Ephesians 6:13 (NKJV)

A lifetime of oppression, hurt, anger, depression, and all those nit-picky little things that go with it will not necessarily leave you all at once. But one by one, they will begin to dissipate. When they do, replace them with the Word of God. Hide it (memorize) in your heart (Psalm 119:11). Because the enemy will try to dredge it back up. It may come in the form of thoughts. It may come through people, family members and "friends" who try to say, "Well I know what you're really like." No, they don't. You know that. God knows that. And so does the enemy. Don't give him a toe-hold. Don't let him drag you back into the trenches. You've been liberated by the Living God. Stand! And when you've done all you can do stand! Let Him be your defense, and never be offended again.

# Revelation to Revolution
**June 8**

I spent the majority of my growing up years trying to please everyone. When I couldn't, I became depressed, often closing myself up in my room and existing in a make-believe world that I created. Inside this world, everything was perfect. Like Alice in Wonderland I lived "in a world of my own." I created this world when I was very small. As any little kid would do, make-believe was something that was okay to do. All little kids use their imaginations and it's wonderful. But my world grew up with me. I made my own rules. I lived in this made up world whenever I didn't have to appease someone in the real world, and frequently to escape the real world.

What I mean by that is that in order to function in the real world, I plastered a smile on my face, said all the things people wanted me to say, and acted the way my family wanted me to act, which was controlled and subdued. I couldn't be upset by something that happened at school or at home because I was told that it was my fault anything negative happened to me. I had no support.

This may not make any sense to you at the moment. You may be thinking that I'm a bit weird, or that I'm crazy. On the contrary. You see, in my make-believe world no one put me down. No one made fun of me. No one laughed at me. No one said hurtful words to me. In a world of my own, I was pretty. I was funny. I was just the right size. Everyone loved me. Everyone wanted to be my true friend. I had control.

This is exactly how the enemy keeps us in slavery to ourselves, our sins, and his lies. And yes, he does lie to us. If he can keep us down, he keeps us from progressing and from moving into the ministry and the relationships that the Lord wants to place us in. Many, many times we believe those lies and it keeps us from the happiness that God wants to see us in. But let me tell you something I've learned: Satan only has the power that you give him.

Here's how I know:

In Isaiah 14:12-14 it talks about the fall of Lucifer (yes, that's his real name). It talks about how he fell, and it talks about how he wanted to be higher than God. But he fell. In verse 16 it says, "Those who see you will gaze at you, and consider you, saying: "Is this the man who made the earth tremble..." What does that mean? It means that one day we'll realize, wait a minute, is *this* the man who made us shake with fear? Is this the one who caused us so much pain? Satan is lower than we are. He was one of the angels in heaven, but he got "too big for his britches" and God cast him out.

Hold on a second, he was an angel? Yes, and angels have no power other than the power God gives them to do the things He tells them to do. Look what Hebrews 1:5-7 (NKJV) says, "For to which of the angels did He ever say: 'You are My Son, Today I have begotten You'?" And again: "I will be to Him a Father, and He shall be to Me a Son'? But when He again brings the firstborn into the world, He says: "Let all the angels of God worship Him."

So Jesus is higher than the angels, has more power than they do. And when we accept Jesus as Lord and Savior, we become joint heirs with Him. So that means that Satan, the enemy, has no power over *me*. Hallelujah! There it is. When I realized this, I had a revelation. It's as if a light bulb went on in my head. When that happened, it began a revolution in my heart. No more will anyone drag me down with unkind words. No more will I be told, "That's stupid!" or asked, "What do you want to do *that* for?" when friends or family hear about the ministry God has called me into. No more will the enemy drag me down with negative thoughts, or my past failures, or my past in general. That is gone. Now I use my past to show others how God brought me out of it. Yes, I lived that way for years in a constant state of oppression (control) because I thought I wasn't worth the salt I put on my french fries. But you know what? I'm worth more than that.

I have begun to resist the enemy. I stand up and I say, "Get behind me, Satan!" And he has to leave. The moment you say "No," Satan has to stop. He cannot stop you. Take an active role in your life now and actively oppose the enemy. When you feel you are being dragged down and you think you have no way out, you are becoming a slave to whatever you choose to obey. For years I chose to obey those who told me that I'd never amount to anything because this is how I was taught. I was destined to be fat, I was destined to be just like my mother and grandmother. Well let me tell you, my mother died from cancer at age forty-eight and my grandmother sat in a rocker/recliner getting larger and larger, and more and more bitter and hateful. Did I want that? No. I refuse to become that. I am not my mother. I am not my grandmother. I am me. I am Shelley! I am a daughter of the Living God and He has called me out, and set me apart for His service. With all the breath that is in me, with all the strength He puts in my fingers to type, I am going to use it. My revolution has begun! Hallelujah! Praise the Lord! (Can you see me jumping up and down, waving my arms?)

God has been calling me into this ministry for years. I could hear Him, faintly across the waves of my turmoil. Faintly from the depths of the pit I was in. But Glory to God, He pulled me out of that pit and placed me in the spot where He wanted me. It was as if He were saying to me, "Okay, you've been in there long enough. You've made an effort to come out, but couldn't quite get there, so I'm pulling you the rest of the way out. Now go do what I've been calling you to do." Then He nudged me in that direction and away I went.

Yes, I have moments of doubt. I have moments of stress when those ugly, imaginary arguments crop up and those people in my head try to tell me I can't do that. But those arguments aren't real. Those arguments are straight from the pit the Lord pulled me from. Then I say, "No!" and they leave. It's a constant battle, but let me tell you something, the Lord is with me and we are winning. You can win, too. Make your decision to get out there. Have a revelation so that you can have a revolution. Don't be afraid. I spent too many years being afraid. You don't have to be, either. Don't give the devil any more authority. You have the authority. By the power that God gives you, you have the authority to cast out the enemy, too. Use it.

# Get Rid of Your "BUT!"
**June 9**

When God healed me of the many years of oppression, offense, un-forgiveness, bitterness, and whatever else it was that I was harboring, He also began to work on getting rid of my "but." No, not my backside. Not my derriere. My "But." You've got a "but" too. Your big 'ol "but" is padding between truth and the lies of the enemy.

> "I know I need to forgive that person BUT..."
> "I know I need to pray more BUT..."
> "She asked me to forgive her BUT..."

Get the picture? For many years, I had a "But." I'm still not completely rid of it, though it's a lot smaller than it used to be. Thanks to the Lord doing surgery on my soul, my "but" has begun to shrink. I'm a lot happier, much more peaceful, and a whole lot lighter feeling as the result.

When you harbor ill thoughts for a long period of time, it begins to weigh heavily on you. It will drag you down. It will make you miserable. Bitterness will set in, depression, oppression, fatigue, stress, unhappiness, etc. A whole multitude of ailments will assail you. Believe me, I've been there. I've done it. I've said I wasn't going back, but found myself there time and time again. Why? Because I believed the lies that the enemy was telling me. Oh they were disguised as many things. Conversations from a "friend" who encouraged me in the fact that I was justified in my feelings. Thoughts that would pop into my head disguised as "the right thing to do." And the sad thing is I would also use Scripture to justify myself and my actions. Now, how sad is *that*?

You may be saying, "I understand that, "but" it's just too hard!" No, it's not. It's not too hard. You just don't want to get rid of it yet. You're still dabbling in whatever it is that you don't want to get rid of. You have not made a conscious effort to get rid of it. And there lies your problem. I'm right there with you, because I've been in that position. And let me tell you, this is how you give the enemy the power to control you. Sometimes we say we want to stop doing one thing or another, or that we want to forgive someone, or we want forgiveness for something, but we don't really mean it. Otherwise we'd be on our faces before the Lord confessing those things and asking Him to remove them out of our lives.

"But" what about when we ask and God doesn't remove it? "But" what about when God doesn't answer? How about this: instead of questioning with a "But," get rid of your "but" pull out your Bible and look for the answer, the reassurance, or the guidance you need? Many times we really just want to hold onto our "but" and question God's seeming lack of interest in us. Because let's face it, we really don't want to give up our insecurities, our qualms, or our sins. All we want to do is complain about them, don't we? I know. I was the same way. I wanted to wallow in self-pity, making things look the way I wanted them to look, get people on my side and just wallow. And then God stepped in and *boom*! The Holy Spirit washed over me, doing spiritual surgery on me, getting rid of every negative thing within me including my "but."

You see, I had gotten out of church for a while because of some bad hurts. I had stopped reading my Bible. I had stopped praying, because I didn't have the words. I literally could not think what to say. I knew God wanted me for something, but I couldn't put my finger on it. Then some people invited me to come to a church they had been attending. They told me how awesome it was. I was skeptical, but went. The rest is history. I wouldn't be writing this right now had I not taken someone up on an invitation to go to church. God is moving. God is healing. God loves you right where you are. And He wants to get rid of your "but." The only thing holding you back is you. You have to be willing. You have to ask Him, believe Him, and receive it.

Shelley Wilburn

# God Can Still Use You
**June 11**

When God told Jonah to go to Nineveh, he ran. Moses murdered someone. David committed adultery. Rahab was a prostitute. Mary Magdalene had seven demons in her. But God still used every one of these people in ministry. So, why couldn't He use you? Who said that He couldn't?

It took me nearly thirty years to figure that out. Through many years of intimidation. Through many years of hurts, depression, being told "women can't preach," and that if you've committed "bad sins" then God can't use you. What exactly were the bad sins? Because when I'd read the Bible, it listed some things, but it never said anything about committing bad sins that would cause God not to be able to use you. In fact, in the book Romans it says that nothing can separate us from the love of God.

"For I am persuaded that neither death nor life, nor angels nor principalities nor powers, nor things present nor things to come, nor height nor depth, nor any other created thing, shall be able to separate us from the love of God which is in Christ Jesus our Lord." ~Romans 8:38-39 (NKJV)

If nothing can separate us from the love of God, then that must mean that God loves us always. And if He could use Jonah, Moses, David, Rahab, and Mary Magdalene, even after the things they had done, (Rahab is even in the lineage of David and Jesus) then why couldn't He use you, too? He can. And He wants to. However some of us, myself included, have to figure it out the hard way. Of course, Moses took the hard road too, as did Jonah and most of the other people in the Bible. Jesus drove seven demons out of Mary Magdalene before she began following Him. But follow Him she did! You see, we are all pieces of the puzzle God is working on. Every puzzle piece is needed. Every puzzle piece is unique. And every puzzle piece fits into the unique spots that the Lord wants them to fit into. Including you.

Although I got saved in 1982, I didn't learn much about being a Christian, much less following Christ nor serving Him until around 1999. When I became part of a Christ centered health program and began doing Bible study and learning Scripture by memory, I began learning things about God that I didn't know. But it took even more time than that before I really began serving Him and making Him Lord of my life. I'm a slow learner sometimes.

May I encourage you today to not ask for anyone's approval for what you do for the Lord. After I had some very godly people pray for me, helping me find the freedom in Christ that I'd been searching for, I found a freedom, peace, excitement, and a ministry, that had been waiting for me for thirty years, maybe longer. Oh, I'm so glad that God is patient.

I knew I was saved. But I didn't realize that He could use even me. This is what the devil did to me. But God can still use me, and since I've sent the enemy packing, I can now focus on what God wants me to do. You can, too!

Shelley Wilburn

# Detour on the Road Trip
**June 12**

A journey is a trip. Some trips take a few days, some take longer. Some journeys can last several months or even several years. Many journeys last a lifetime. I don't know how long my journey is going to last.

It has taken me many long and suffering years to get to where I am now. And it only took God one evening to send me in the direction I needed to go. How exciting that we have a Heavenly Father who loves us so much that He is willing to wait, take His time with us, and never give up on us. I love that "never give up on us" part.

When I began writing in my journal about forgiveness it was because everywhere I turned, there was a song, or a commercial on TV, or a devotional, or something that mentioned forgiveness. It dawned on me that the Lord might just be tapping me on the shoulder wanting me to pay attention. So I began writing about it. I literally started writing in my journal on February 29, 2012. I thought you know, that might come in handy one day. I might just need to write a book about forgiveness. Then Joyce Meyer came out with her book on forgiveness, *Do Yourself a Favor...Forgive Yourself* (Faithwords, 2012).

You see, every time I would see someone come out with a book or story about something I had an idea to write about, I thought I couldn't write about it then. Someone "stole" my idea! No, they really didn't. But in my situation at the time, I believed the enemy's lie that God really didn't call me to write. So I would lay aside my ideas. But here's the really nifty part: those ideas never left me. They stayed and floated around in my mind, wanting me to do something with them.

Here I am now. I'm a little late, but that's okay. My journey to forgiveness has truly begun. I kept thinking about it, wondering how I was going to write about it but I felt blocked by a big, brick wall. However, God broke through that wall so I could continue on my journey.

The enemy will set up road blocks along your journey. He will cause you to take detours that you didn't intend to take. But if you'll read the Map (the Bible) and ask God for directions, you'll have less road blocks and less detours. My mistake was in not asking for directions. I put my Map down and decided I could drive on my own. Not that everything was my fault. Because many of the things that were preventing my journey were due to my past. There were things in my life; intimidation, fear of what others would think or say about me or to me, fear of rejection, etc. that I had no idea were there. But God has been bringing things to mind so that I can purge them from my life. You have things in your life too. Little things. Things you have pushed to the far, dark corners of your mind. Things you don't want to deal with. Things that didn't seem important, but they are important. If they are preventing you from continuing with your journey, they're important enough to be dealt with.

I'm asking you right now to bring them out and let the Lord handle them for you. You may need to call in some Godly people who can pray with you. That's okay. That's what we're supposed to do. Pray for each other.

"Is anyone among you suffering? Let him pray. Is anyone cheerful? Let him sing psalms. Is anyone among you sick? Let him call for the elders of the church and let them pray over him, anointing him with oil in the name of the Lord. And the prayer of faith will save the sick, and the Lord will raise him up..." ~James 5:13-15(a) (NKJV)

Are you ready to continue the road trip?

# Sticks and Stones
**June 12**

*"Sticks and stones may break my bones, but words can never harm me."*

Remember that little ditty? Well, it's a lie. We learned it when we were kids so that when other kids picked on us, or called us names, we could sing-song it back to them to let them know they didn't hurt us. But they did, didn't they?

Years of hurtful words, by many people, pushed into that lock box in the dark corners of your mind. The box no one can open unless they say something hurtful to you. Only now it's so full that it can't contain everything you want to hide in there and it's actually not even in the corner anymore, but out in the middle of your mind. Those little hurtful words have festered into very sensitive little sores within you and people step on them every day. The least little thing can set you off. You've prayed about it, but you can't seem to get rid of those hurts. What can you do?

*"Therefore humble yourselves under the mighty hand of God, that He may exalt you in due time, casting all your care upon Him, for He cares for you."* ~1 Peter 5:6-7 (NKJV)

That's what you do. You cast it upon the Lord. He can handle it. He wants it. Casting it upon Him, literally throwing it rids you of the many burdens you've been trying to carry and deal with. But you were never meant to deal with them. Did you know that? Jesus told us to bring everything to Him. If He wasn't serious, He wouldn't have said it.

"Come to Me, all you who labor and are heavy-laden, and I will give you rest. Take My yoke upon you and learn from Me, for I am gentle and lowly in heart, and you will find rest for your souls. For My yoke is easy and My burden is light." ~Matthew 11:28-30 (NKJV)

I carried one burden after another for years upon years. I thought I was giving everything to Him when I prayed, but before long, my words seemed to hit a brick wall. I literally could not figure out why I couldn't get rid of all those things that people had said to me over the years. They were suffocating me. All those things in that crammed box were spilling out, making me sick, both mentally and emotionally. It was time for a cleansing.

"Call to Me, and I will answer you, and show you great and mighty things, which you do not know." ~Jeremiah 33:3 (NKJV)

The night I was healed I had many people praying for me and over me. When I cried out to the Lord, He most definitely answered me. He began a healing within me. Then He began showing me many things. Let me tell you, when God promises you something, you'd better get ready, because He definitely does not go back on His Word. Since beginning this journey to forgiveness, God has shown me great things and mighty things, and wonderful things, and He continues every day to show me something else. Every day He gives me a new story to write. Yes, I remember many of the hurtful things that have been said to me. But those things have no effect on me now. Instead, I'm using them to get my message across to you who are hurting, so you too can begin to heal.

"Therefore, if anyone is in Christ, he is a new creation; old things have passed away; behold, all things have become new." ~2 Corinthians 5:17 (NKJV)

Shelley Wilburn

# Stop Listening to Lies
**June 13**

I learned a very important lesson. Just now. Oh, I've know about it for quite some time. But then I actually heard it spoken out loud by someone else and the light bulb came on. The lesson; when the devil starts talking to you in your ear, you can speak out loud out with your mouth and he'll have to shut his. Never run at your giants with your mouth shut. Remember that verse of Scripture that says, "Resist the devil and he will flee from you" (James 4:7, NKJV). It's truer than you realize.

How many years have you lived in oppression? How many lies have you believed? You aren't pretty enough. You aren't thin enough. You don't clean your house right. You don't raise your kids right. You don't dress right. Blah, blah, blah, blah! Over and over and over again. It's never enough, is it? I heard those same things for many years. I lived it many more. When some of the people who spoke those things to me were no longer present, their words were. I kept hearing their hurtful words like a broken record in my mind. It got to a point where I would purposely avoid doing dishes, laundry, or housework of any kind because when I would those hurtful words would pop back in there and make me miserable. Before I could finish a job, I had worked myself into a nervous wreck. So, I avoided it. If I didn't do the dishes, I wouldn't hear those voices of shame. But if I didn't do the dishes, they would pile up, and before long the broken record would start saying other things. "See? You'll never amount to anything." Lies, lies, and more lies. All of them straight from the devil. All of them straight from hell.

For years, you've been listening to the same broken record that I have. Of course, your broken record may sound different than mine, but the theme is the same: to keep you in the past and from moving forward. This is oppression, control.

It's time to stop looking at our past and look toward our future. So what if those things happened to you in the past? Are you going to continue to let the enemy keep you in that, making your life miserable until you die? I say no. God wants to prosper you, not harm you. He wants to love you and for you to love Him. But more than that, God wants to do something new in and with you!

"Behold, I am doing a new thing! Now it springs forth; do you not perceive and know it and will you not give heed to it? I will even make a way in the wilderness and rivers in the desert." ~Isaiah 43:19 (Amplified Bible)

The night I asked for more of Jesus, more of the Holy Spirit, and surrendered to what He wants me to do, a wellspring of stories bubbled up within me and the words kept coming, and coming, and coming.

What is it that God has gifted you to do? Do you have a heart for caregiving? Do you love to work with children? Do you love working with teenagers? Are you a good baker, love taking things to others to brighten their day? Give it to God, give yourself to Him and watch what happens! Don't let anyone tell you that you can't do it. Don't let anyone tell you it's a stupid idea. Because if God has called you to do it, He will also equip you to do it and make a way for you. So stop listening to the enemy. Say out loud right now, "No!" Tell the devil, "That's enough!" He has to shut his mouth and leave you alone. Do this every time you hear something negative whispered in your ear. Before long, you will begin to feel peaceful. You will begin to get excited about what the Lord wants you to do. You will be happy to do it and can't wait to get going every morning.

"Do not be conformed to this age, but be transformed by the renewing of your mind, so that you may discern what is the good, pleasing, and perfect will of God." ~Romans 12:2 (HCSB)

Set your mind and keep it set.

# Deflating Balloons
**June 14**

How's your journey going? Have you had any bumps in the road? Had any bridges to cross or "One Way" street signs posted on you? How about any detours? Yes? Congratulations! You're going in the right direction. Believe me, I'm not laughing at you. I'm laughing with you even if you aren't laughing yet. Seriously though, it's not funny when the enemy throws his darts at us, is it? But he does throw them, and any time we can continue with our journey and get past what the enemy throws our way, I stand and applaud you. I'm so proud of you, and I rejoice with you in continuing your journey regardless of what is placed before you.

"Consider it a great joy, my brothers, whenever you experience various trials, knowing that the testing of your faith produces endurance. But endurance must do its complete work, so that you may be mature and complete, lacking nothing." ~James 1:2-4 (HCSB)

Trials along the journey are normal. Of course we're going to have them, it's a given. But here's some good news; if we are prepared, the trials won't seem so bad. In fact, they will seem so ridiculous that we laugh them off. And let me tell you, the funniest thing to me is when someone tries to trip you up and you don't trip, but instead smile, or laugh it off. I have experienced that firsthand. When we don't take offense to those who try to insult us in front of others, drag us into a tete-a-tete, or even resist when they try to get us to gossip about someone not present, immediately they become confused and you can literally see all the hot air blubber out of their balloon. You just took all the fun out of their game. Instead, you have fun and enjoy yourself along with everyone else while your would-be oppressor sits and tries to figure out what just happened. That's God...and I love that!

I'm thinking of a particular incident in my last paragraph. Let me just say that when a particular person at a gathering started out being nice to me, then stated loud enough for everyone to hear, that they never see me anymore it didn't work. I laughed it off. I never asked, "What do you mean by that?" nor did I fall quiet, as I used to do, which would elevate my angst and cause me to not have any fun. This time, I was the one who had fun and my oppressor sat quietly for a while.

I'm not saying to be mean or rude to those who try to oppress you. I wasn't mean to anyone. What I am saying is to be nice to them. Love on them. Let them know that you have been delivered from your abuse and that it is not okay for them to try to treat you rudely, insultingly, condescendingly, accusingly, or harshly anymore.

"If your enemy is hungry, give him food to eat, and if he is thirsty, give him water to drink; for you will heap burning coals on his head, and the Lord will reward you."
~Proverbs 25:21-22 (NLT)

I used to jokingly say that I liked that "heap burning

coals on his head" part. But you know what? That is really sad. It's sad that it takes such a drastic measure to get through to someone who wants nothing but to attack you spiritually, mentally, emotionally, in public, or however. How do we heap burning coals on someone's head? By being nice to them. By loving them. I have literally seen someone get mad because I'm being nice and having a good time instead of facing off in confrontation with them. I have been called petty because I live by what the Bible says. Hey, I'm following Jesus. Come with me. You'll be happier, too. Sadly though, many people won't. They rather enjoy being where they are and think that you are crazy for what you are doing and being where you are. Let this be an encouragement to you today. You can and will go farther in healing your mind, emotions, and spirit when you trust the Lord for everything within you. I can't say it enough, and you'll just have to go along with me here, but it's the truth.

When the Holy Spirit was working on me it was such an overwhelming cleansing, a spiritual surgery of sorts. I was lifted, delivered, and healed of those many years of people saying negative things to me to keep me down. Depression, intimidation, anxieties were all gone. I was healed. You can have it, too. Trust me. Just pray and ask for it. Believe it. Receive it. Then bask in His glory, because you have begun your journey to forgiveness.

Shelley Wilburn

# Past Is Past
**June 16**

Isn't it awesome how when Jesus saves us, we become a completely new person? He can take all of our sins and cast them as far as the east is from the west. He can cleanse and heal us from old hurts and scars. He can make us as fresh as a field full of lavender (I happen to like lavender). We truly are a new person. God remembers our past no more. Too bad everyone else doesn't forget, too.

"As far as the east is from the west, so far has He removed our transgressions from us." ~Psalm 103:12 (HCSB)

Too often, our friends and family refuse to forget our mistakes and our mishaps. We are dragged through the mud by statements like, "Don't give me that 'Holy Roller' attitude. I know what you're really like," or "I know who you really are."

Well, no, you don't. The ones who want to slander you are holding onto that one moment in time when you slipped up, or didn't live for Christ, or maybe didn't even know Him at all. To them, it doesn't matter if it was twenty or thirty years ago, or twenty or thirty minutes ago. Your accusers will remember the smallest detail of your life forever. But to God, if we have asked Him to forgive us, it's forgotten. We often allow those we love though, to control us, keeping us in that black hole of the sin that God forgave us for. They simply refuse to allow us out, always pushing us back down into it. We allow them to because simply put, we just don't know how to get over it and forgive ourselves, or may not even know that we're allowing it to happen. Who cares what you did wherever or whenever? If you have asked God to forgive you He did. The past is in the past.

Many times the reason we come under so much attack by our family and friends is because, 1) Our relationship with Christ makes them uncomfortable; and 2) they simply refuse to let go of the past. Yes, it is a little more difficult when dealing with family. They watched us grow up. We like to live in the past, remembering the "good ol' days," and unfortunately remembering the mistakes others have made. Of course there is a third reason which is the other person just doesn't know that they are being hurtful. They say things to you that they truly believe to be helpful, never knowing or seeing the damage they are causing until it's too late.

One of the hardest things I've ever done is to separate myself from certain people, friends or family. Frankly, I don't like who I become when I'm around them. They belittle me, trash talk about me (whether I'm present or not), and always try to trip me up by asking me question after question about the things I do. And when finally I get flustered and mess up, they are the first ones to attack. "Well I thought you were a perfect Christian?" You can't pass that off as "just joking." Yes, I am a Christian. And the beauty of being one is that I know I'm forgiven of my sins. It doesn't mean I'm perfect.

"Therefore, if anyone is in Christ, he is a new creation; old

things have passed away, and look, new things have come. Everything is from God, who reconciled us to Himself through Christ and gave us the ministry of reconciliation."
~2 Corinthians 5:17-18 (HCSB)

    How sad that people only want to remember what you did "back when," but can't accept who you are right now. Honestly, they're missing the best part of you.
    Don't listen to them. Be who you are in Christ. Enjoy the new you, and don't let anyone push you back into the pit.

# Take Off Your Mask
**June 18**

Is your life a masquerade? Have you been oppressed for so long that you're living behind a mask, not even knowing who you are anymore? I was like that, too. For years I lamented over "wish I coulds" and "what ifs," never knowing that there was something wonderful lying just under the surface. The problem was that I didn't know how to tap into it and bring it forth to move myself forward. In addition to that, even if I could tap into it, I was scared to death of what would happen if I did! Who was going to get mad? Who was going to confront me? On, and on, and on...

The night that God healed me everything that was lurking deep within me came flooding to the surface. And guess what? It was everything that I already knew, everything that I am, and everything that I've always wanted to be...plus more! I found things within me that I had no idea that I was capable of doing. All of a sudden, I could look people in the eye, I could speak to people without fear, and I could smile again, and laugh. I could write with a flowing power that had eluded me before. But the most amazing thing that I discovered was that I had a compassion for people and could actually talk to them without fear. I was finally able to take off the mask I had been wearing for years and get rid of it. I don't need it anymore. Besides, it was broken so it literally fell off.

What kind of mask are you wearing? Is it one of fear?

Oppression? Depression? Verbal and mental abuse? Sexual abuse? Drug addiction? Alcoholism? Whatever mask you're hiding behind, let God remove it from you. When you go to Him, fully trusting Him and allowing Him to heal you from the inside out, He will remove that mask you wear and crush it, never to be worn again. I promise you that. God knows the real you. He made you. And He has a purpose for you. The enemy has had you in so much turmoil, using the very people you know and love to keep you down and keep you from being the wonderful you that God made you to be. I know. I've been there. And now I'm out, and I'm throwing you a lifeline. Grab on, we'll move forward together.

I'm not saying that you'll never come under attack again from your oppressors. But here's the really cool part: When God heals you, those attacks will roll off you as if you're covered in some kind of anti-adhesive. Because you are. Jesus has covered you and has become your protective sealant. Those fiery darts thrown at you from all sides just bounce off. Of course you can hear them. You may even feel them hit you. But they have no effect on you anymore, because when God fixes something...He does it up right. So let the enemy try. He won't succeed. Because if you truly accepted the healing of God, there isn't a person anywhere who can put a mask back on you.

# Finding Your Treasure
**June 22**

Have you any idea how rich you are? You may not think so. You've been beat down for so long that you don't think that there's anything good inside you. But there is. If you know Jesus, there is a light shining within you. You are a clay jar with cracks and that light will shine through the crack, peeking out and letting others see that hey, there is definitely something about that person. I know this from personal experience.

"We now have this light shining in our hearts, but we ourselves are like fragile clay jars containing this great treasure." ~2 Corinthians 4:7a (NLT)

You see, when God healed me a change happened within me. I knew the Lord. I had accepted Him a year before I got married. But that's about as far as it ever went. I was saved. What more did I need to know? A lot more, apparently. Sometimes though, we have to get to a certain point in our lives where we are actually ready for God to use us. And God has to get us to that certain point in our lives when the clay is ready for the Master's hands. I was at that point the night God healed me.

I had been praying, others had been praying, and a very godly man prayed with me, invoking the help of the Holy Spirit, and when he touched me, the Holy Spirit washed over me and my knees buckled and I literally went fell in the floor. It all sounds so unreal, doesn't it? My point is this: when I prayed and received the Holy Spirit more fully into my life, He began to work on me and filled all those cracks in my clay jar. I have a lot of cracks in my pot too, but the Lord turned the lights on and now I'm a beautiful light, shining out to those of you who are hurting, depressed, and have been beaten down for as long as you can remember. And I want to help you find the light switch within you and turn it on, too.

"The Lord executes righteousness and justice for all who are oppressed." ~Psalm 103:6 (NKJV)

You were made for so much more than what others are telling you, dear lovelies. So let's do a little emotional exercise. It won't hurt a bit and you'll be glad you did it. Right where you are I want you to pray and ask the Lord to remove the shackles of oppression from you. Believe in your heart that He wants to heal you. Say, "I believe it." Then receive it. Say, "I receive it." Say, "In the name of Jesus!" If you truly mean it, He will heal you. He will remove it from you, and you will be healed. You can be healed right this minute. Matthew 21:22 (NKJV) says, "And whatever things you ask in prayer, believing, you will receive." The peace, the peace of mind, the rest, actual rest for once in your life, the tension removed, and many other things that you wouldn't have dreamed could happen, can and will. Your clay jar will be filled with even more treasure.

If you have been oppressed by others, I want you to cry out to the Lord for healing. I want to pray for you. Because someone took the time with me, I will take the time to pray for you. God can heal you from it. He can use you. He loves you so much and has a purpose for your life. But you have to be willing to let Him and willing to stop letting others drag you down and control you. We have no control over what others say and do. But we do have control over what *we* say and do.

Let's start fresh every morning with the Lord, and allow Him to show you which way to go. He has given me a freedom and a ministry to help others. I have the Lifeline. Would you like to grab hold of it and find your treasure?

Shelley Wilburn

# Do It Afraid
**June 23**

"The fear of the Lord is the beginning of wisdom."
~Psalm 111:10 (NKJV)

For years I feared the Lord. The Bible teaches us and it's even stated throughout, "Do not be afraid." The fear we are taught in the Bible though means that we are to have a respect for the Lord, be in awe of, to revere (be reverent to) Him. In my instance, I was outright afraid of Him. Because I feared my parents, their wrath if I did something wrong, I let that fear spill over to my heavenly Daddy, thinking much the same about Him. It wasted so much time.

I thought God was this huge ruler, sitting on a throne (the Bible says He sits on a throne (Hebrews 1:8). I thought He was waiting for me to mess up so He could *zap* me. I would hear how we were supposed to work for the Lord and how if we didn't work then our faith was dead (James 2:17). I would always timidly serve my part wherever I was needed. Always knowing in my heart what I was supposed to do. No one understood that though. I would hear things like, "Oh, we really need you here" or "We've been talking and we think you should do this." I would never say a word. I would always comply, quietly going to do the job no one wanted, quietly wondering why I couldn't do what I knew the Lord called me to do. I was afraid.

I was afraid to step out. I was afraid to stand up for myself. You see, I had been conditioned to always do what I was told to do. If I didn't, I would get into trouble and the consequences were devastating. If I got into trouble at school just plan on being in trouble at home, only more severely. And somehow I always brought it on myself. I'm still trying to figure that one out. Intimidation and manipulation. It filtered into my adult life. If I didn't obey my husband, then the consequences were going to be devastating. Oh wait a minute...my husband is loving, kind, a man of God, someone who loves the Lord and loves me, too. He never raises his voice. He never raises his hand to me. He never cuts me down. He never does any of the things I was told a husband would do if a wife didn't obey him. But a marriage isn't supposed to be like that anyway. A marriage between a man and woman is supposed to be loving, kind, patient, gentle, and above all respectful. I had all those things in my husband, yet I was still afraid. Not of him, but of what "might" happen. I lived in fear every day when I didn't need to.

How hurtful it must have been for him. I have apologized to him and do you know what he has said to me? "Honey, I love you."

Until the Lord finally healed me of the years of hurt that I was packing deep inside me, I lived in a constant state of indecision, confusion, and fear. None of that is of God, none of it.

"For God is not the author of confusion but of peace..."
~1 Corinthians 14:33 (NKJV)

Over the years, my oppressors have had many different forms; family members, church members, friends, friends of friends, friends of family. One would think that I would have overcome this sooner rather than later, but I finally did. Let me tell you, although I'm healed, I'm still learning what to do with my healed self. It's a whole new ballgame out there now. People who know me have noticed that there's a change. Something is different in me. There's a new confidence. There's joy. There's a light in my eyes that wasn't there before. The major fear is gone and replaced with the confidence that once was missing. Oh, I'm still afraid, but not of getting in trouble. I'm afraid in an excited nervousness of what the Lord is teaching me and having me do. This time though I won't let fear control me. This time I'm forging ahead. I'm going to do it afraid.

If the Lord has given you a task, don't sit and work yourself into a tizzy. The enemy would like nothing better than for you to get so afraid that you chicken out before you can complete your task. So here's my encouragement: *Do it afraid.* If you do, I promise you that the Lord will meet you as soon as you take the first step in faith and the rest will be easy-peasy.

# Setting Boundaries
**June 24**

Someone once said, "When we give in to fear we always run away from something we should be confronting." For years I gave in to fear. I allowed it to come in and control my life. I allowed it to build a fortress around me, and I ran every chance I got from the things I needed to confront and take charge of. Sadly, I feared almost everything and in so doing caused many people to have very little respect for me. I lived in a constant state of oppression. I didn't stand up for myself because I didn't want to rock the boat.

My childhood fear of getting into trouble if I wasn't obedient to everyone carried over into adulthood.

"Now I urge you, brothers, to watch out for those who cause dissensions and obstacles contrary to the doctrine you have learned. Avoid them, for such people do not serve our Lord Christ but their own appetites. They deceive the hearts of the unsuspecting with smooth talk and flattering words."
~Romans 16:17-18 (HCSB)

I neglected to set boundaries for those in my family, for my friends, and acquaintances. Now, there are those who, when you stand up to them, will use that as ammunition to attack you more. These are the people who only cause divisions and problems, and these are the people from whom we need to distance ourselves.

By distancing yourself from controlling people it often causes them to lash out at you more. However, by staying away from them, you have set your boundaries. You have let them know that, 1) God is first in your life; 2) You will not allow them to control your life; and 3) You will not allow them to use you as the chopping block to make themselves look better. You do not have to listen to them, and whatever they say about you will eventually come back on them.

"I tell you that on the day of judgment people will have to account for every careless word they speak. For by your words you will be acquitted, and by your words you will be condemned." ~Matthew 12:36-37 (HCSB)

People who are oppressive or controlling speak the true nature of their hearts. If they try to control others with manipulation, intimidation, and oppression, these are people to stay away from. Before you totally remove yourself from them though, you need to make sure that they know where you stand. Make sure that you explain to them, "Look, I love you but I will not allow you to put me down and call me names no matter how much you say you are joking. It is hurtful. If you want me to respect you, you must respect me in return. If you can't accept this, then I cannot be around you."

I will tell you up front, with some people you can do this. Others, you cannot. You know the people in your life better than anyone. Sometimes, to confront those who oppress you only causes more arguments and more ridicule for you. Some of them will have no idea that they've been hurting you. It might just be a healing for the both of you.

No matter your situation, always put Christ first and trust Him to help you through your situations. It's always good to pray first, then confront. Let the Holy Spirit give you the words to say. Do it gently, in a godly manner, and in love. Set your boundaries regardless of how others treat you. They will know where you stand, and the Lord will back you up.

Shelley Wilburn

# Shields Up!
**June 28**

I was talking to D.A. about being under spiritual attack. I was preparing to take a trip to meet someone to do a radio show and tell my story. I had waited two weeks for this day to come, and now just two days before I was to go, the attacks had begun. But this time, something amazing and wonderful had begun to happen. Instead of those negative thoughts, imaginary confrontations and conversations stirring up my feelings of oppression once again, whenever they would try to pop into my mind, immediately they would bounce off and away.

At first this was a little confusing to me, because they began as they always did. Only this time they weren't as clear for me to hear. They sounded sort of muffled. It helped me to identify them more quickly and in doing so, I could shut them down. When I would shut them down (a mentally uttered, "Stop it" or a verbal "No") I could literally feel them bounce off of something within me.

It wasn't until later in the evening, when I was talking to D.A. that it came to me; Shields! My shields were up. I remember saying, "It's like on *Star Trek: Next Generation* when Captain Picard yelled, "Shields up!" There is literally a force field around me so that when those oppressive thoughts and comments try to come in, they immediately bounce off." Of course, D.A. just looked at me. He's not a "Trekkie." But

I knew what it was, and talking about it out loud helped me to identify it. It was my faith.

When you put your faith and trust in Jesus, believe Him for your protection, and you are truly working to follow Him, you will have shields and they will always be up. Here's how I know...

"Stand therefore, having girded your waist with truth, having put on the breastplate of righteousness, and having shod your feet with the preparation of the gospel of peace; above all, taking the *shield of faith* with which you will be able to quench all the fiery darts of the wicked one. And take the helmet of salvation, and the sword of the Spirit, which is the word of God..." ~Ephesians 6:14-17 (NKJV, emphasis mine)

When someone tries to drag you down because of what you are doing, your shields will protect you from their hurtful words. I have had enough hurtful words to keep me down for the rest of my life. But Hallelujah! when the Lord set me free from that, He put my shields up and as long as I'm following Him, they'll stay up.

So let the enemy fire at me! Let people try to drag me down. I don't need Commander Data to keep an eye on my shields. I have the Holy Spirit. As long as I stay in God's Word (the Bible), and keep talking to Him (in prayer), my shields (my faith) will remain intact. If I start to feel them slipping, or feel a hole in my shields, I will go to God, not Geordi La Forge, and God will strengthen me and restore my shields.

Shelley Wilburn

# Mass Communicating
### July 1

Surfing on Facebook one morning, I saw that Melody Miller, one of the morning radio personalities from then WIBI radio station, posted a question. I answered that question and it set off a chain of events that would end up taking me to be on the radio. The question was, "So what has God been teaching you lately?"

I couldn't not respond to that. I was also a little bit afraid of what others might think if I did post. Now, right there my former fears were surfacing. Instantly they were removed and this soothing, peaceful, very small voice said, "Answer her." So I did. My comment went something like this: "So much that I had to start a website to contain it." I know I put more in there than that, something about being taught forgiveness and being healed of many years of oppression; however just that much was enough to send Melody to my website. Within a few short minutes, she had made another post, telling people to go read my story. She had posted a link to one of my stories, and within another few minutes I received this comment: "Girl, you need to come do the show with me!" I quickly responded, "I'd love to!"

As soon as I clicked "send" I thought, "What have I done?" By that evening, the date for me to be on A Positive Start to Your Day with Melody was set.

Before that however, the most amazing things were happening around me and within me. Gone was the nervousness. Gone was the anxiety. Gone was the worry that usually accompanied me when I was about to do something "big." In their place was a confidence in myself that I'd never had before. I never worried one time about the show. I never worried about what I would say. I never worried about what Melody might ask me or say to me. There was a peace, a calm, and an assurance that I had never had before. It was all God. It was all the healing that He had given me. It was all still there. It was all still working.

I have come to realize since my healing experience that when God heals you, He keeps you healed. There's no going back. There's no, "Oh you just messed up so you have to start over." There's none of that. Healing is healing and once healed you're sealed. It's the truth. God healed me, then called me out to do the thing I had been praying for years that He'd let me do. Write. It was there the whole time, but I had a lot of junk in the way. Now I was preparing to tell it on the air to a huge listening area. And I was perfectly calm about it.

The drive to Carlinville, Illinois, would take about two and a half hours, I would stay overnight in a motel somewhere and make sure I was at the station at 7:20 AM to do the show with Melody. D.A. drove me and we had a very good time getting to talk and spend quality time together.

I have a little confession to make. When I got up the morning of the show, my stomach was a little queasy. But shortly after we left the motel to drive over to the radio station, I received a private message from my aunt that read: "The devil doesn't want you to break through because he knows that if you do, you will become a world changer...Joyce Meyer post just now." Immediately my nervous stomach went away. I knew that the Lord had sent me to deliver my story to someone out there who needed encouragement and the enemy didn't like it.

Upon arrival, Melody met me at the door with smiles and an abundance of energy that was catching. We hit it off right from the start. She got me acquainted with the station, giving DA and me a tour of the building. Then she sat me down in front of this huge microphone and told me, "We go on the air in ten minutes. Would you like a bottle of water?"

Before I knew it, Melody was welcoming me to the show, telling her listeners that her "new friend" was in the studio today, and we were going to be talking about my amazing journey. Then she asked me a question and away we went.

I can't tell you exactly what I said or what she said. But it wasn't long before the phone on her side of the counter started blinking. We had a caller. Then another caller. I was truly amazed by God. Because I gave everything I had into His hands, praying that He would prepare Melody, prepare me, and prepare the listeners, whoever they may be. God gave us the words to say. He gave the listeners the ears and the hearts to hear. And before long, it was ten o'clock and the show was over. Where did the time go?

Everyday life isn't always doing a radio show. I certainly did not go there with the intention of bringing attention to myself. But I did go there with the intention of bringing attention to God and how He can turn your life around if you'll just trust Him. He did it for me.

You can hear the Podcast of the morning radio show by going to this link: http://soundcloud.com/radiomelody/shelley-wilburn-podcast

# Healing Rain
**July 2**

I often speak to the Lord while standing on our front porch which looks out toward the wooded area behind our property. If I get there early enough in the morning I can see some deer making their way out of the woods, over to the cornfield which sits right next to us. The woods are home to many a wild animal. I know this because my son-in-law Jake once strategically placed "deer cams" at the end of the field and let me tell you, we have some pretty amazing pictures.

Just the day before, I was jumping around on the front porch, yelling "Hallelujah! Thank you, Jesus!" while the rains came pouring down. That is until I got pelted with a couple small pieces of hail, at which time I ran inside. But I was just so excited that God had answered my prayer for rain that I wanted to tell him.

A day after the round of thunderstorms came through I stood in a puddle of cool rain water at the end of my porch. Looking out over the field, I spoke to the Lord thanking Him for the healing rain that He gave us and various other things. Often I find myself talking, and talking, and talking and then I realize that maybe He has something to say to me.

I held my Bible close to my heart as I prayed. I realized that there was something in there that the Lord wanted to say, so I opened it and this is what I read out loud:

"To You, O Lord, I lift up my soul, O my God, I trust in

You; Let me not be ashamed; Let not my enemies triumph over me. Indeed, let no one who waits on You be ashamed; Let those be ashamed who deal treacherously without cause. Show me Your ways, O Lord; Teach me Your paths. Lead me in Your truth and teach me, For You are the God of my salvation; On You I wait all the day. Remember, O Lord, Your tender mercies and Your loving kindnesses, For they are from of old. Do not remember the sins of my youth, nor my transgressions; According to Your mercy remember me, For Your goodness' sake, O Lord." ~Psalm 25:1-7 (NKJV)

    Reading it out loud was proclaiming God's Word, His promise over me. As I read, I realized that He was reminding me that He had heard me. He saw me lift up my soul to Him. He saw me put my trust in Him. He also reminded me that He knows full well the ones who have treated me badly, and He will deal with them in His time. They won't triumph over me, by putting me down or making remarks about me behind my back. Those things are trivial and of no importance to me, nor to the ministry that God has called me to do. But He also showed me and reminded me that the sins I've committed in the past are just that. In the past. Every day He is teaching me this and helping me to move forward in a new light...His Light.

    A month before I was beaten down, withdrawn, emotionally, mentally, and spiritually a mess. I had been verbally abused by various people throughout my entire life. The only person, other than the Lord, who knew what my potential was, was my husband, Don Athen Wilburn, aka D.A. Thank God he never gave up on me. Thank God that *God* never gave up on me.

*Walking Healed*

God hasn't given up on you, either. He wants you just the way you are. He has something for you to do. But you have to trust Him. You have to bring everything within you to Him and just be honest. Be honest with yourself, and with God, and just tell Him; "Okay, I can't do this my way anymore. It isn't working. You know that. So here I am. Forgive me Lord, and use me for whatever it is that You've called me to do."

Don't let others keep you down any longer. Come out of that black hole you've been in and play in the healing rain of God's love.

Shelley Wilburn

# Freedom
## July 4

Independence Day. When we celebrate the independence of our nation, I always love the fireworks display, especially the ones of our town. Of course, I just love watching fireworks anywhere, including the big ones! I love the bright colors, the crackling of the sparklers, and even those stinky, sulphur-smelling smoke bombs and their brightly colored smoke. I loved buying those when I was a kid and setting them off in the yard to see how many colors I could get. Those were some fun times growing up.

Can you imagine what would be happening in our country if our troops hadn't fought for our freedom? I'm so thankful for, and proud of, all of them.

I'm also extremely thankful for the spiritual freedom that God gave me. Since being healed I can see things in a whole new light. Gone are the anxieties of the past. Gone are the hateful barbs of those who have picked at me for years. And gone are the feelings of worthlessness that have been drilled into my head by those who wanted nothing but to insult and keep me down.

This might sound harsh, but there are those who cannot feel good about themselves unless they are putting someone else down. These are the people I have to stay away from. Some of them are family, some friends, some even women I once went to church with. I may love many of them, but I limit my time with them because to be around them for any length of time only causes stress and physical illness. Some of these people I stay away from completely.

I've talked about it before, but this is a healing process. Just because I'm healed of the oppression doesn't mean my life is perfect. It just means I'm on a new journey. This is my "Journey to Forgiveness." Some people aren't going to like it. Some will retaliate. Just like when our troops are fighting for the freedom we get to enjoy in the United States. Our adversaries in other countries don't like it, so they retaliate. It's basically the same way with our spirituality. Our enemy, the devil, is constantly looking for someone to devour (destroy). That's why we have to be on alert so that we can fend him off.

"Be sober, be vigilant; because your adversary the devil walks about like a roaring lion, seeking whom he may devour. Resist him, steadfast in the faith, knowing that the same sufferings are experienced by your brotherhood in the world." ~1 Peter 5:8-9 (NKJV)

The good news is that I have a God who is bigger than all of that. He has promised me that He will be with me every step of the way. I may have to walk through some rough spots, but I am now better equipped to handle it. There will be no more oppression for me. I may get attacked verbally, but those are just words from people who don't "get it." I don't have to be around them. I have other things to do and can't waste my time letting someone try to trip me up.

Let me tell you what the devil did to me. For many years

of my life there has been someone constantly putting me down. I'm not whining about it, I'm just stating facts. I never knew how to handle it, and therefore allowed others to bully and control me, never defending myself. But let me tell you what the Lord did for me: He came in and took all of that emotional and mental oppression and intimidation from me and gave me a fresh start. I stand before you today healed, cleansed, and ready to do what the Lord has called me to do: Help others who are suffering the same thing.

    I am happy. I am free. I am a brand new person. Freedom isn't free. Someone gave his life so that you and I can live in a free country. Jesus gave His life so that you and I can live eternally. I hope you all have an eternity with Jesus, celebrating the independence He gave us.

"But may the God of all grace, who called us to His eternal glory by Christ Jesus, after you have suffered a while, perfect, establish, strengthen, and settle you."
~1 Peter 5:10 (NKJV)

# Make Up Your Mind
**July 6**

Every day is a new adventure in my journey. I learn new things and can literally see how far God has brought me in such a short amount of time. I wonder how I made it this far without ending up in a padded room somewhere, but then realize that although I suffered many years of mental and emotional abuse, God was there the whole time. He also had a plan for me, and He knew just how much I was capable of handling before He got me to where He could mold me into what He needed me to be.

You may be wondering, if God is so loving then why did He let these things happen? It's not that God wanted me to suffer. He wanted to heal me, for me to walk in a ministry He was calling me into. The problem was that I wouldn't let Him work in me. I didn't know how. I was afraid then of what others might think or say. I would quietly worship God on Sunday, but allow others to dictate how I acted Monday through Saturday and I hated it the whole time, living in misery, but showing the world a smiling face. I literally hid in my suffering, for years, and years, and years.

Today, I watch others doing the same things. I watch as one person after another says something about God, praising Him today then tomorrow speaking with the foulest language or crudest remarks. Still, a few days later, when their lives have taken a turn and something bad comes along they wonder why God is doing this to them. They flit back and forth between God and their misery, never making up their minds.

"Now above all, my brothers, do not swear, either by heaven or by earth or with any other oath. Your "yes" must be "yes," and your "no" must be "no," so that you won't fall under judgment." ~James 5:12 (HCSB)

For years I made excuses for the mess my life was in. I had no idea that what I felt in the pit of my soul was the work of the enemy. There was literally a ball of "yuck" inside me that was churning and making me more miserable. I had no idea that it was years of the oppression, verbal and mental abuse, and bullying that I had endured, clear into my adult years.

An *excuse* is a *lie* disguised as a *reason*.

What I needed was for God to take care of me. I needed a major pruning, and some of the things coming out of me needed to be thrown in the fire.

One night, they were. The night God healed me He removed every hurt, every foul word ever spoken to me or from me, and He began to patch me up. I was transformed in that one evening and given new wings to fly. I was given a destination and pointed in the right direction to get there. Then God gave me a little push, like giving a little bird a lift to fly, and off I went.

"But those who trust in the Lord will renew their strength; they will soar on wings like eagles; they will run and not grow weary; they will walk and not faint." ~Isaiah 40:31 (HCSB)

*Walking Healed*

You too, have a calling from God. Believe it or not, you do. He has a plan for you, He has a job for you, and you need to believe that right now. Stop letting the enemy convince you that God is doing these bad things to you. He's not. He loves you very much. So let your "yes" be "yes," and your "no" be "no," (HCSB) and stop playing on the fence. Instead, make up your mind to let God mend your fence and let Him give you the wings to fly.

Shelley Wilburn

# Moving Forward
**July 9**

It's one thing to be healed of years of oppression and intimidation. The peace that flows through me is amazing. God is more real than He's ever been before. My senses are more attuned to what's going on around me. Sleep comes more easily and it's more refreshing. I'm able to rest once again, without little niggling remarks from the past running through my head, ruining what sleep I would have got. It's easier to wake in the morning. In fact, I do so with anticipation of a new day. It's actually a welcome thing to wake before the alarm, so I can go out to the porch and spend a few quiet moments alone with God and tell Him how wonderful He is, thanking Him for the healing once more, and reading His Word in anticipation of what He wants me to know for this day.

But what do I do after the healing? When the moment is long gone and I've come down off the cloud I was floating on the first few weeks. When I've had a couple of undesirable moments with stressful people though I handled it well, what am I supposed to do now? Is God still listening to me? More importantly am I still listening to God?

It's time to move forward. Walk healed.

God healed me for a reason. To help others. To minister to others. He set me on this path of restoration after healing me. He has given me a new purpose in life and a new ministry. I can do nothing more but move forward with it, following Him.

When God heals you of an issue, or several issues you've had buried deep within your soul, you come out of it into a new light. At first it's hard to see things around you because it's so bright and clear out here in the open. But gradually things begin to adjust. You're at a sort of standstill because there's a newness within you. A getting-used-to-this-new-thing kind of feeling that takes a little getting used to. There's excitement. There's a new awareness. Peace, joy, happiness, and laughter, all come back to you.

There are also remembered hurts. There are those little aggravating voices, trying to sprout old hurts back into life. But instantly they are squashed back into the pit from whence they came. There is no more dwelling on the issues of the past, because let's face it, they are in the past. It's a new day and you're a new you.

So what happens when you finally adjust somewhat and the newness wears off? That's when the moving forward begins. Taking those baby steps, walking steps, then running steps forward. Stay in prayer. Keep reading your Bible. This will keep you grounded. This will help you move forward. We have to move forward in our journey if we are to be successful. If we stay where we are, we end up going back into the black hole. There are always going to be those people who try to keep us from moving forward.

"Devote yourselves to prayer; stay alert in it with thanksgiving." ~Colossians 4:2 (HCSB)

Every day I get up and start my day talking to the Lord.

Shelley Wilburn

I open my Bible and ask Him what He would have me to know today. I just open my Bible and wherever it opens, I read. What I read in there after I've spoken to Him often deals with the very things I've talked to Him about and right there is my answer.

Let God ground you in His presence, in His Word, in His conversation, in everything. When you get grounded, you'll be able to move forward.

# Wisdom In Reconciling
**July 11**

While reading a daily devotion one morning, not only did the title speak to me, but a few things within the devotion as well. In the devotion, it talked about which is the right thing to do when someone says or does something that hurts us. Stay quiet and pretend like nothing is wrong, or confront them with how wrong they were? What is the godly response? I began to wonder, "God, are you trying to tell me something?"

When God healed me a great weight lifted from within me. I was able, for the first time in many years, to truly feel forgiven and to feel forgiveness for others. But what about down the road, when I have to face my oppressors again? What do I do when I'm faced with someone who has always said negative things to me, or bad-mouthed me? What do I do then? How do I stay honest, yet maintain my integrity?

We can't go into a confrontation with self-righteousness on the tips of our tongues. It is very important we seek the wisdom of the Holy Spirit before we even open our mouths because we know there are people in our lives who are going to cause issues. So we hand them over to the Lord, and we ask for wisdom to be able to handle the situations that arise.

"But the wisdom from above is first pure, then peace-loving, gentle, compliant, full of mercy and good fruits, without favoritism and hypocrisy." ~James 3:17 (HCSB)

By focusing on God's wisdom and the godly wisdom He gives us, we will be able to invoke a peaceable reaction to those who seek confrontation. By reacting in a godly way with love, peace, a kind word, etc., we can show our intimidators we aren't going to fight with them.

Sometimes that will be enough to diffuse the situation, though sometimes our intimidators are looking for a fight. But if we have prayed about the situation, truly seeking God's wisdom, He will give us the peace-loving, gentle, response we need. We will be able to show mercy to those seeking intimidation and confrontation.

Still, there will be times when reconciliation with someone just doesn't come. It is very sad when this happens. There are those whom I have prayed for, for years. The reconciliation has not come. There have been many confrontations, all ending in the other person becoming angry, while I sit calmly, trying to negotiate. They become agitated, yelling and throwing curses my way. It never ends with a calm reconciliation of our relationship. I have not gone into it blaming the other person, but trying very hard to reconcile. Nonetheless, there is never a calm restoration. These are the people that I must, for obvious reasons, stay away from. It breaks my heart.

Reconciliation is a two-way street. It's a give-and-take. In this situation, the right thing to do is to give it to the Lord and let Him provide the wisdom, discernment, and the reaction that I need. If you have someone in your life that you have not been able to reconcile with, seek the wisdom of the Lord. Pray and ask Him for guidance. Hopefully one day you will be able to reconcile. It's never too late to try.

"If any of you lacks wisdom, let him ask of God, who gives to all liberally and without reproach, and it will be given to him, But let him ask in faith, with no doubting..." ~James 1:5-6(a) (NKJV)

Shelley Wilburn

# When Friendships Fail
**July 13**

I was thumbing through my journal one evening. I had started this journal on February 29, 2012. I titled it, Forgiveness because it was a topic that kept popping up everywhere I turned. It even invaded my thoughts. I decided to better pay attention and take notes because there was no telling where this was going to lead.

I had written about how I needed to pay attention because I believed the Lord was telling me something. I even wrote; *I'm going to take a lot of notes because I believe this forgiveness thing is what is going to end up being what I write about. So in admitting that, as I embark on this journey, Lord Jesus, please guide me, be with me, open my heart and my mind and soul to not only be able to give forgiveness but to receive it and then to be able to tell others about it so they too can be helped.*

Little did I know that this small, but profound prayer was not only heard, but it was prophecy of what God was about to do in my life. It was three months later that God healed me.

Since then, here is the proof of that healing. You have been reading it. It has become my journey. I write because I know that there are people out there who are suffering inside like I was. You have family, friends, and people you love who intimidate and control you, who are mad at you for one thing or another. And you must find a way to have forgiveness for them, try to restore the relationships, and move out of the pit you are in.

Restoring relationships is a difficult adventure. I say "adventure" because of all the things we go through in order to restore a lost one. Though many times we cannot restore it, and we just have to move on, continuing in prayer for the one who will not be moved.

As I write this, I have someone in mind who has seen it as a great injustice to herself that I didn't do something that she believed in her heart I should have done. Various things prevented me from following through. But before twenty-four hours had passed, she was angry with me and no longer speaking to me, nor was she any longer my friend. I tried to apologize to her, to no avail. Phone calls, text messages, and emails went unanswered. The last time I saw her, she would not acknowledge me, nor speak to me. The hate and unforgiveness radiating from her, along with the judgmental attitude were palpable. Others even noticed it and asked me what had happened. I declined to explain.

How sad she must be, carrying that around with her, disguised as justification. My heart is heavy for her, and yet I wonder just what kind of a friend she really was if she can hate me so thoroughly because of one mistake. I wonder if she really had been my friend at all. I also wonder if I had been a very good friend to her. If I had been, shouldn't I have helped to teach her a little better about forgiveness and the importance of not holding a grudge? Thinking back though, at the time I too, was carrying the weight of years of hurt, oppression, and angst within me that I didn't know how to deal with. This is still no excuse. However, since being healed, I can see the damage I have done. What can I do now but pray those mistakes I made with others will be forgiven. It is not solely my fault for some of the things that have happened in the past. But I shoulder much of the blame in not trying to fix it sooner.

It does not settle things to continually drag up the past, trying to get over it. Yet many times, the people we surround ourselves with thrive on the past mistakes of others. They take great pleasure in dwelling on the negative, keeping us in a constant state of strife. I spent way too many years in that stage of continually bringing up past hurts, trying to "talk it out." I would try to reason my way through it, trying to find my justification. My motto was, "God can do more to them than I ever could, so I'm not even going to deal with it." This is a wrong mindset. This attitude will get you into more trouble. Not with others, but with God. To drag up past issues and hurts will only cause more pain.

For years I lived in a spiritually bi-polar state. Being in ministry for many years with my husband, I had to function as a person who did not have issues. I would help and guide someone going through depression or someone dealing with an intimidating relative or friend, all the while dealing with the same issues myself. It was easy to give prayer and advice to others, yet I was using myself as the stepping stone for others to climb up and out while I stayed in.

Since my healing, my journey has been one of learning, of growing, and of laying to rest the things of my past. If I can do that with those with whom I have unresolved matters, that's another victory. If I cannot resolve issues with them, then I must move forward and pray that someday they too, will find the forgiveness that I have found.

# Beauty for Ashes
**July 16**

There was a time I thought my life was nothing but a pile of ashes. I had come so far in depression, oppression, and intimidation that I truly think there was nothing left but the ashes of my despair. Has your life come down to that, too? Let me encourage you today. God wants to give you beauty for your ashes. He wants to turn your ashes into something beautiful. For all the years you've suffered intimidation from others. For all the years you've suffered depression as the result of the oppression pressing you down into the pit of darkness that surrounded you. God can take you out of it and turn your life into the beautiful thing it was meant to be.

"The Spirit of the Lord God is upon Me, Because the Lord has anointed Me to preach good tidings to the poor; He has sent Me to heal the brokenhearted, To proclaim liberty to the captives...*To give them beauty for ashes*..." ~Isaiah 61:1-3(a) (NKJV, emphasis mine)

You are meant for so much more than what you've been allowed to believe of yourself. I don't care who told you that you couldn't do something. God says that you can. Want to know how I know this? Because I've been there. I've been sitting in the dark pit of ashes that my life was becoming. I have suffered oppression. I have suffered depression, manipulation, intimidation. I can't tell you enough how many people have come in and out of my life who have felt it their duty to belittle me, ridicule me, insult me, or demanded I change one thing or another about myself because they didn't agree with something I said or did. I always endured it because I was raised that you did not dispute what someone else says to you. But what I wasn't told was that everyone is not always right.

I didn't know about the love of Jesus. I had no idea that He wasn't some kind of dictator, on His throne, waiting to zap me with a great punishment for the bad stuff I've done. Suffering and punishment come in various forms, yes. But just because someone is going through a bad spot doesn't mean that God is punishing them. Sometimes it's a test of faith. Sometimes it's an attack of the enemy. Sometimes it's both. What did Job do to deserve all he went through? Nothing. His faith was being tested. He wasn't being punished. And God ultimately restored him. But my point is that many times people want to focus on the bad stuff and subsequently blame God for their bad lot in life. They want to believe that God is ultimately going to punish them for their sins...even if or when they've been forgiven.

"I'm just waiting for my punishment," they may say. Well, okay you go right ahead and wait. But I'm going to rejoice in the love and forgiveness of the Lord. People who have lived a life of constantly being intimidated by others who believe they have the right answers will know what I mean here. God is a fair God. He's just. He's also jealous, and His wrath is something that I don't want to endure. But God's wrath is coming for those who never accept Him and never turn from the bad stuff they do.

"If My people who are called by My name will humble themselves, and pray and seek My face, and turn from their wicked ways, then I will hear from heaven, and will forgive their sin and heal their land." ~2 Chronicles 7:14 (NKJV)

I didn't enjoy suffering depression, anxiety and panic attacks. I also didn't enjoy always feeling like everything was my fault and I was always to blame for everyone else's problems. I suffered. Plain and simple. Job suffered so long that he began to question his faith. Have you done the same thing? Have you suffered something that is controlling your life for so long that you're beginning to wonder if God even cares about you? I've done that. I truly thought that God hated me and was going to zap me with cancer, just like my mother, and kill me off. Now that is a sad mentality. This is how the enemy tricked me and caused me to believe his lies. I became so afraid of God that I literally thought that He had left me. So one day, He showed me just how that would feel.

I believe that God pulled back just enough to allow me to feel what my life would be like without Him. I have known Him for so long that I just didn't realize that He was there. When He pulled back, the devastation, loneliness, despair, and hopelessness that overcame me was so overwhelming, it literally caused me to cry out for Him in a panic; "God! Where are you?! Please don't leave me!" Instantly, those bad feelings disappeared and were replaced with peace, comfort, and love. God had been holding me, just like when your kids were small and they would cry for you in the dark. You were there the whole time, but they didn't know it until you touched them.

It took about four years to come out of that mess. But it took another couple of years before we found a church where we could learn and grow and where Jesus could get ahold of me. That's when God said, "It's time for a complete healing." That's when He did "Spiritual Surgery" on me and healed me of every bit of that mess.

Not everyone's story is going to be like mine. But there are people out there who are suffering needlessly because someone somewhere told them God was punishing them. Those are not God's plans for you at all. He has good plans for you and they don't include punishment at all. So why not let Him give you beauty for your ashes today?

"For I know the plans I have for you," declares the Lord, "plans to prosper you and not to harm you, plans to give you hope and a future. Then you will call on me and come and pray to me, and I will listen to you. You will seek me and find me when you seek me with all your heart. I will be found by you," declares the Lord, "and will bring you back from captivity..." ~Jeremiah 29:11-14(a) (NIV)

# Water on the Rocks
**July 21**

Riding our motorcycle through the mountains in North Carolina, we passed many rushing streams and creeks. The water running over the rocks was beautiful. In places it ran quickly, rushing over the various rocks, making little waterfalls. In other places, it ran slower, often just trickling over the rocks. No matter how it was flowing, it was beautiful.

Leaning into one curve, I happened to notice a particularly rocky stream with the water rushing quickly over the rocks. I began to think, the longer that water runs over those rocks the smoother they will become. I thought about how God designed and created that rocky stream and how the water will change the surface of those rocks over time. That's about the time it felt as if the Lord whispered in my motorcycle helmet and said, "I am the Living Water. This is what I am doing with your life."

Wow! How profound a statement, but I understood it. Since He healed me of so many mental and emotional scars, Jesus has been working on smoothing out the rough spots here and there. He patiently works in areas that I have difficulty with, and in areas that are not much of a problem for me. He gently glides over, smoothing away those areas so that I can move on to better things.

I also began to think about how necessary water is in our lives. We need water to live. We drink it to hydrate and heal our bodies, so we can stay healthy. We use it to cook with, to work with, and to wash with. Water is necessary for life. We also need Jesus to live. He hydrates our souls, heals our bodies, keeps us healthy, and washes us clean of our imperfections and sins.

Jesus is able to heal us in an instant. But often He uses our imperfections and our rough edges to help us learn and grow. The things in our lives that cause us pain most often are the things the Lord uses to help us help others. If we have gone through it, we can help others who are going through it, too. This is why He has given me the ability and boldness to write about my experiences overcoming intimidation and depression.

Living that way was not fun, and I often wondered why I was suffering and no one else could see it. Jesus saw it and saw the opportunity to use me to help someone else. When He healed me, Jesus, the Living Water, rushed through me, first washing away the unnecessary things. Then, He replaced those rough, jagged edges with a smoothness, giving me something to use to show others that yes, you too can be healed and still survive.

As the water in the mountains runs over the rocks in the streams, smoothing out rough edges over time, Jesus does the same thing with us. Sometimes the water is soothing. Sometimes it is rough and rapid. But no matter which runs through your life, if it is Jesus the Living Water, you can bet that you'll come out of the rapids a beautiful, smooth, stone shining like a gem.

# Overcoming Fear
**July 26**

"There's no need to fear! Underdog is here!"

My favorite cartoon when I was three; *Underdog*. I don't know why this was my favorite cartoon, but it was. I loved the music, the characters, and everything about Underdog. Especially the fact that he always yelled, "There's no need to fear!" just before he flew in to save the day. As long as Underdog was here, there was no need for fear. But as I got older, I realized that Underdog was just a cartoon, and there were things in my life that did cause me fear; things that I did not know how to deal with.

At age fifteen, I had fallen into the "black hole" of depression so deeply that even a cloud in the sky would scare me to death. I was afraid of everything; storms, clouds, people, school, church. I was even afraid that the world was going to end and I was going to be left behind, all alone, with no one. But I had no idea why I thought the world was going to end, or even why I should be afraid of being left behind. At that time, I didn't know God, nor did I know that He loved me and didn't want to hurt me, but instead He had a plan for me.

Not knowing how to get out of the black hole is scary enough. But fear is something that the enemy puts on us, not God. God does not want us to be afraid. Throughout the Bible, we are told many times not to fear. If it's in there so much, then don't you think God is serious about us not being afraid? I think so, too.

"For God has not given us a spirit of fear, but of power and of love and of a sound mind." ~2 Timothy 1:7 (NKJV)

When we come to know the Lord, He gives us power and love, and He takes hold of our thoughts, giving us peace. He does not give us fear. I did not know this for such a long time. It's a shame really, how long it took me to figure it out. I spent many years under such depression, never knowing that the answer to my issues was within praying distance.

However, because God works all things together for good (Romans 8:28), He used the issues buried deep within me to help me find my calling and my healing. He has helped me conquer my persecution and pain and He has set me on the course to helping others become conquerors, too.

"Yet in all these things we are more than conquerors through Him who loved us." ~Romans 8:37 (NKJV)

This is what the Lord did for me. He can do it for you, too. While Underdog saves the day in the cartoon world God saves the day in the real world. There's no need to fear! GOD is here!

# Label Makers
**July 30**

We are a society of labelers. We have a label (or name) for everything. I think sometimes we put labels on things and people so we can better understand them. But often we put labels on things and people so we can avoid them. Many do it to be hurtful.

It's that whole "You say tomato, I say tomahto" thing. But which is right? Are they both? Or is one more correct than the other? One says one thing. Someone else says another. Both think they're right. So what's the point?

The point is this: We need to be careful what we say and do because that will eventually catch up with us.

"Do not be deceived, God is not mocked; for whatever a man sows, that he will also reap. For he who sows to his flesh will of the flesh reap corruption, but he who sows to the Spirit will of the Spirit reap everlasting life."
~Galatians 6:7-8 (NKJV)

I have been labeled many things throughout my life. Some were very hurtful. But those who have labeled me have not really known me. Because of their own opinions, or something they were told by someone else, they gave me a label. Many of those labels I carried with me for years.

The night God healed me there were a lot of things that happened to me. I have labeled it many things myself, not knowing exactly what to call it. But the fact remains that I was healed, this much I know.

When God healed me though, He not only removed all those things, but the Holy Spirit came rushing in and filled all those places in me that had been causing so much damage before. He removed intimidation, oppression, depression, hurt, anxiety, and the old labels that had been placed on me over the years, and He replaced them with more of the Holy Spirit. It was like what happened in Acts chapter two. Sure, I was a Christian before it happened. Afterward I was still a Christian, but a healed one, a different one, a better one. Not perfect. Just different. I had (and still have) a new outlook, a new lease on life, and a new calling.

Have you been labeled? Are you bogged down with so many that you don't even know who you are anymore? Let me encourage you to have a face-to-face encounter with God. Throw everything to Him and ask Him to heal you, and let go of the past things that have caused you so much hurt in your life. Let Him remove your labels and give you the only one that matters: "Child of God."

"Fear not, for I have redeemed you; I have called you by your name; You are Mine." ~Isaiah 43:1(b) (NKJV)

# Learning to Let Go
**August 1**

In my journey to forgiveness, I have found that sometimes things aren't what they seem to be. It's that way in all of life's little quirks I guess. Many times we say we have forgiven, yet we're still holding onto one little thing or another. We haven't learned to let go.

Often I hear things like, "I'm not very good at letting go of things," or "I haven't mastered the art of releasing the past." I wonder then, how do those people have forgiveness in their hearts? They don't. You can talk all day, saying you've forgiven so-n-so for one thing or another, but the fact remains that if you can't talk about it without it upsetting you or making you angry, then you haven't really let go of it.

If you begin to release past hurts and pains, then you'll experience the joy and freedom God intends for you to have.

I know I speak of the things of which God has healed me. It was a lifetime of being told my ideas were stupid, that having my feelings hurt were my fault, or just the hopelessness of not being encouraged to excel at anything. The intimidation brought on by various people throughout my life weighed heavily on my shoulders. And while I talk about being healed of it, I don't actually talk about each individual infraction done to me. To do that would dredge up old wounds, old hurts, and old "junk" that has been healed within me. The fact of the matter is this: I've been healed.

The night God healed me the Holy Spirit rushed in to

fill the holes that all the former hurts had caused. It's like when you get a cut or scrape. Immediately blood rushes to that area, clotting it, and scabbing over so that the skin underneath can heal. That's exactly how it worked inside me. All those abrasions throughout the years had left holes. The blood of Jesus rushed in, filling each hole, and the Holy Spirit scabbed them over, beginning the healing process.

"Simply put, forgiveness is the decision to cancel a debt."
~Andy Stanley (*It Came From Within!*, 2001)

There are many people in the world today who are hurting. Whether by the hands of someone else, or by their own unwillingness to let go of past hurts and pains. The issue with forgiveness is that we have to be willing to let it go. We can say we forgive all day long. But until we actually let it go, nothing will ever change. God wants to heal you. You have to let go so that He can. If you say you're having trouble with it, then you aren't ready to let it go. When you do though, you will experience such a sweet release that will completely turn your life around.

# No One Like You
**August 3**

I once read an article titled, "The Comparison Trap." It talked about how we, as women, often fall into the trap of always comparing ourselves to other women and always falling short. It got me to thinking and I realized that, I never fell into the Comparison Trap at all. I was born into it.

When I got saved, I struggled with the fact that I didn't have to perform in order for God to love me. I had no idea of the freedom He just gave me. All I knew was that I got saved and that I was going to heaven someday. That's all I thought there was. Little did I know.

The sad thing is that it took me the better part of twenty-nine years to finally figure out that it doesn't matter what I look like, what I wear, how I do my hair or makeup, or even how thin or how fat I am. God loves me for me. I am His design. So of course I'm not going to be like anyone else! I shouldn't compare myself to anyone else. I am me! I am a one-of-a-kind, no-one-else-like-me, He-broke-the-mold-when-He-made-me person. So are you!

"Exhibit God with your uniqueness. When you magnify your Maker with your strengths, when your contribution enriches God's reputation, your days grow suddenly sweet."
~Max Lucado (*Cure for the Common Life*, 2005)

You and I don't have to have anyone's approval for

what we do. God has given each of us special gifts. Some of us know ours, some of us don't yet. But the fact remains that if you are living and breathing, God has something special for you to do. You can't get anywhere by comparing yourself to the next person. It's up to you to find your talent and make use of it.

"For as we have many members in one body, but all the members do not have the same function...Having then gifts differing according to the grace that is given to us, let us use them..." ~Romans 12:4, 6(a) (NKJV)

My life isn't perfect. It never will be. I will grow and learn from now until I stand before Jesus with my accomplishments and say, "Here they are." Knowing that I'm doing it for Him, to help others heal from their hurts and grow closer to Him, I pray that what I do here is pleasing to Him. Because everything I do is for Him.

Have you fallen into the trap of comparison? Do you find yourself looking at others and thinking that you aren't as good as they? Not everyone is called to write, or preach, or blessed with artistic talent. Sometimes we're called to just be a good listener, or take care of someone's child, or run errands for a sick neighbor. Let me tell you something: you are good enough! You are designed by the Creator of the Universe. You are one-of-a-kind. God has a plan for you and has instilled in you something special. He doesn't make mistakes. I encourage you to step out in faith. Trust Jesus to lead you in the direction He is calling you. When you do, you will find liberation, and a peace that you never knew you could have.

# Cracked Pots
**August 12**

I must confess...I'm a bit cracked. Well, maybe not a bit. A whole lot! There are a lot of cracks in my persona. Many I would like to forget, to cover up, and to put something over so no one else can see them. But do you want to know something? If we are honest with ourselves, we're all cracked. And the beauty of that is—God uses cracked pots.

Every time someone says a hurtful word to you, every time someone is taken advantage of, every time a friend or relative hurts us in some way shape or form, it causes a crack in our person. Whether our self-esteem, feelings, confidence, or even our physical bodies get hurt, mentally, emotionally, or physically, it creates a scar of some sort. These are the cracks I'm talking about.

In 2 Corinthians chapter 4, the Apostle Paul talks about stuff like that. He had been beaten, abused, locked up, and persecuted for his belief in Jesus. Before he came to know the Lord, he was called Saul, and he persecuted Christians for their belief. So he knew all about abuse. In verse 7 he says, "But we have this treasure in earthen vessels, that the excellence of the power may be of God and not of us" (NKJV). The best part of this passage though comes from the next few verses:

"We are hard-pressed on every side, yet not crushed; we are perplexed, but not in despair; persecuted, but not forsaken; struck down, but not destroyed..." (2 Corinthians 4:8-9, NKJV)

Though people may say hurtful things to us, though they may try their best to destroy us physically, mentally, emotionally, we are not destroyed. For years, I thought I was utterly destroyed. I had so many cracks in my "earthen vessel" that I thought I couldn't be of any use to anybody.

Here's the good news: God is the Great Physician. He's the Healer. He's the One. He's the Alpha and Omega, Beginning and End. He is the author and finisher. And the night He healed me, He finished my suffering. He took me, in my cracked pot, my earthen vessel, and He began filling those cracks with His love, healing, and Holy Spirit. He is now using this cracked pot to encourage all of you.

It's like when we use a cracked flower pot for a plant. When we water that plant, the water seeps out of the cracks and spills out all over the place. Well, in this cracked pot, Jesus has filled me so full that the Holy Spirit is spilling out all over the place!

I had no idea when I started writing at the age of twelve that I would someday be writing to help encourage others. I had no idea I would even encourage others to use their cracked pots to let the light of Jesus shine through to help other cracked pots. So I'm a cracked pot! God is still using me, and He can sure use you, too.

# Don't Miss the Point
**August 24**

Having been intimidated and oppressed for the better part of my life, it was a revelation to me when I realized that I didn't have to take that from anyone and that the Lord actually had a purpose for me. He has a purpose for you, too.

You may be thinking that being intimidated and controlled is a way of life. Not just with family, but with friends and those around you in various positions. However, when the Lord steps in and says, "You don't have to live that way," it sets off a chain of events that your oppressors (controllers, intimidators) don't, and won't understand. They may take a very bold step to try to keep you from progress. This is very dangerous ground for them. It's a form of bullying. For instance, they'll intimidate the person beside themselves in order to control them. They stay in control, but you have been manipulated into submission. Some people enjoy being in control.

"Pride goes before destruction, and a haughty spirit before a fall." ~Proverbs 16:18 (NKJV)

Living under the control of people who only continue to put you down, whose words and actions keep you from living, actually prevents you from having the life that God intended for you to have. It also makes you physically, mentally, and emotionally sick. It can lead to having to take medication for anxiety, depression, stomach problems, high blood pressure, acid reflux, pills to help you sleep, or to wake up. I have been on many of them over the years.

Even though I had accepted Jesus, like many, I missed the point. The "point" is that Jesus can, will, and wants to heal you. Missing the point for years and years, I suffered clinical mental depression. I suffered panic and anxiety disorder. I also suffered migraine headaches. My weight fluctuated; I would lose a lot of weight, get thin and begin to feel better physically, but I worried that I was still fat, worried about what others thought of me, and initially would gain the weight back, plus more. At this writing, I was heavy. I take medication for a hiatal hernia to prevent having acid reflux. All of this stemmed from a life of oppression and intimidation. Stress causes many health problems and I lived in stress for the better part of forty-seven years.

I would hear things like, "You need to pull yourself up by your own bootstraps and move on!" For those who do not understand, or have never suffered under the heavy hand of intimidation, it's not that easy. Intimidating people pose their questions and comments in a condescending and insulting way which causes fear, anxiety, causes you to question yourself inside with, "What do I do?" I'm still challenged with various people who still try to intimidate me this way. I don't have connections with them every day but when I am, I have to pray for the Lord to help me have boldness. I also practice being assertive.

In the book of John, John the Baptist was preaching and teaching, baptizing people and telling them about Jesus. The Pharisees, (the religious leaders) were the intimidators, the oppressors. They asked him questions, trying to intimidate him.

John answered the Pharisees with prophesy out of Isaiah,

"I am the voice of one crying in the wilderness: Make straight the way of the Lord..."
~John 1:23; Isaiah 40:3 (NKJV)

But the Pharisees totally missed the point.
John went on to say,

"I baptize with water, but there stands One among you whom you do not know. It is He who, coming after me, is preferred before me, whose sandal strap I am not worthy to loose."
~John 1:26-27 (NKJV)

They wanted to know who John was, what right he had to be saying what he was saying. John told them who Jesus was and they missed the point.

Many will miss my point. I am not worthy to be writing what I write. But I also know that I have been healed of the oppression and intimidation I suffered. And the Lord has given me this venue to write what I do in order to help many of you who have suffered, or are suffering the same things. Like John, I am now the voice of one crying in the wilderness.

I'm here to tell you that Jesus is here for you. He wants to heal you. He wants to give you a fresh start. You do not have to suffer anymore. Believe He will heal you, and He will. Ask Him. But whatever you do, don't miss the point.

Shelley Wilburn

# From Duh to Aha!
**August 28**

Does your mind ever wander? Mine does. It usually gets me into trouble, too. Because when I'm idle, that's when the enemy begins to pick at me, bringing to mind many things that I would rather just leave alone. What's worse, to me anyway are the ridiculous conversations that pop into my mind that aren't even real, that try to take control of my emotions. Some make me angry, some cause anxiety, some remind me of the divisions that a few people have caused. And many remind me of how I let them hurt me. This is how the enemy keeps you intimidated and oppressed. By bringing up your past and reminding you of ways people have abused you.

I was having those particular thoughts one day. They were starting to cause me a bit of anxiety and fear. But all of a sudden it dawned on me what was happening and I literally spoke out loud, "Duh!" It was as if the Lord spoke to me and gently revealed this: "I told you I would take care of it. You need to trust Me." Well, duh again!

"The Lord knows the thoughts of man..." ~Psalm 94:11(a) (NKJV)

I instantly realized that I had been allowing the enemy to bring back into my mind things of my past and things that

*Walking Healed*

hadn't even happened. I was playing the "What If" game and I should have just said, "Lord, this bothers me and I know you are going to take care of it, so I'm giving it to You."

"Search me, O God, and know my heart; try me, and know my anxieties; And see if there is any wicked way in me, and lead me in the way everlasting." ~Psalm 139:23-24 (NKJV)

We often have to have a "Duh" moment before we can have an "Aha!" moment. For some of us (like me), we have to have several "Duh" moments before we realize that we are not capable of handling things on our own. When we realize that is when our "Aha!" moment arrives.

Mine was when I realized that I had forgotten to trust the Lord and began to worry how I was going to handle being around someone who usually causes me stress and anxiety. As I stepped into the shower to get ready for my outing, that's when it hit me. "Oh, duh! I'm sorry Lord for not trusting you with this. I know you are going to take care of this situation and I apologize for not paying more attention. Help me to do better." Instantly, the anxiety and stress left, and I was able to enjoy the day.

Prayer, no matter how simple and short has instantaneous effects. Have you had any "Duh!" moments in your life?

# Grace Who?
**September 18**

Sometimes I just don't get it. I mean, I've heard it for so long, attribute it to my salvation experience but actually giving it well, sometimes I just don't get it. Grace. In the past, grace, to me was always a "who" not a "what." Grace, who? Where is she going? What is she going to do when she gets there? And just where is there?

Then I met Jesus. Thing is, it took me a very long time to really figure out grace. For the longest time I thought "I'm saved. End of story." I literally thought that's all there was to it. However, there's a whole other realm. Not only am I saved, but I have grace, forgiveness, healing, peace, love, joy, patience, kindness, goodness, faithfulness, gentleness, self-control, and the list is endless. When God healed me He taught me that grace is a very special and wonderful gift.

"For the Lord God is a sun and shield; The Lord will give grace and glory; No good thing will He withhold from those who walk uprightly." ~Psalm 84:11 (NKJV)

I get a few devotions in my inbox. A while back, several almost coincided with each other; Max Lucado, Proverbs 31 Ministries, Internet Cafe, just to name a few. Max even had a new book out. Wanna take a guess at the title? *Grace.* Topic of his devotions? *Grace.* Topic of many of the other devotions: *Grace*. I see Facebook and Twitter posts from Joyce Meyer and Joel Osteen. Many of them are about, *Grace*. Okay, okay, I get it! Grace.

Dictionary.com defines grace this way: favor or goodwill, manifestation of goodwill, kindness, mercy, clemency, pardon.

"But He gives more grace. Therefore He says: "God resists the proud, But gives grace to the humble." ~James 4:6 (NKJV)

In my journey to forgiveness I have learned how to forgive those who intimidated, oppressed and controlled me for many, many years. Now that I have figured that part out, the next step is to give them grace. To show them kindness. Show them love. Show them mercy, clemency, pardon. It does not mean that I allow them to treat me badly over and over. I have set boundaries so that doesn't happen again.

But grace is so much more than that in my book. Grace is not only saying, "I forgive you," but it's also saying, "I love you." You may be able to do this in person with some, maybe not with others. And there may be some who are no longer here, who you're just going to have to give grace to their memory. But if Jesus loved us so much to give us his forgiveness, grace and mercy, shouldn't we do the same for others?

Shelley Wilburn

# Do Yourself A Favor
**October 6**

I was thinking about this journey to forgiveness that I'm on. Yes, I'm still calling it a journey. Mainly because it is. That and the fact that in my journey I've hit a lot of bumps, potholes, snags, and detours. I began to wonder what had happened. Where did I make a wrong turn? Why don't I feel like I did when God first healed me? Why am I not doing nearly as well as I was when I was first healed? Did I have a relapse? No. I'm having life, plain and simple.

**Being Forgiven Doesn't Mean Easier**

Did I think everything was going to be sunshine and roses after God set me straight and nudged me in the direction I was supposed to go? Maybe. I'm not sure what I thought. I guess I thought that things would be easier.
Just because we're forgiven, doesn't mean things get easier. It doesn't mean things go back to the way they were, either. Because often times they get harder. We just have the ability to handle them better, that's all. And yes, quite often we will run into someone, or several someone's, who won't understand us. Nor will they want to hear us, or hear our story. And not everyone's forgiveness story is the same.

## Watch Out For Enemy Attack

It's also a time when the enemy sees an opportunity to either bring back up certain things that caused us shame, or bring up things from our past that caused us great shame. False conversations arise. False situations. All of them using something in our past that makes us step back and wonder. One of my problems is forgiving myself. But here's something I learned in a devotion that actually opened my eyes and caused me to take notice.

It's that whole "I can't forgive myself" attitude. Do you realize that in taking that attitude, you are basically telling God that Jesus' death on the cross was not enough? Ouch! How prideful and arrogant we are to take that attitude. Because in Psalm103:12 (NKJV) it says,

"As far as the east is from the west, so far has He removed our transgressions from us."

If I'm not mistaken, the east and west never meet.

Do yourself a favor.

Here's another tidbit of information for you. Author and Bible study teacher Kay Arthur of Precept Ministries International said, "The idea of forgiving ourselves cannot be found anywhere in the Bible." It's not in there. If we sincerely ask God to forgive us, then He does. Period. It's gone. Wiped away. The slate is clean. Why then do we pick it back up and waller it around and stew over it?

So, in this journey to forgiveness, it's not just about forgiving others. It's also about believing that when we ask Jesus to forgive us of our sins, He does. They're gone.

They're not coming back. We need to get over ourselves and get back on track and focus on the truth of what His Word says.

"If we confess our sins, He is faithful and just to forgive us our sins and to cleanse us from all unrighteousness."
~1 John 1:9 (NKJV)

Jesus forgives you. So do yourself a favor and forgive yourself.

# Got Junk in Your Trunk?
**October 9**

Are you a collector of junk? I'm not talking about those lovely treasures we find tucked away in a corner of some antique store. I'm talking about J-U-N-K. Those ugly words someone said to you yesterday, or years ago. Whether from classmates, teachers, family, or friends, those nasty, hurtful things stick with you, sometimes for life. Ugly. Lazy. Stupid. Good for nothing. Mistake. Idiot. Fat. Weird. Worthless. Troublemaker. On and on and on.

I carried many of those pieces of junk with me for years and years. I stuffed them all in a little treasure box in the far recesses of my mind. The trouble was, I stuffed so much down in there that before long, my box became a trunk and it was so full of junk that I didn't even know what was in there anymore. But it sure knew me and it kept me from living the life God intended for me to live. Why? Because the enemy likes nothing better than to make our lives miserable. So I packed and packed. I had too much junk in my trunk.

"Stay alert! Watch out for your great enemy, the devil. He prowls around like a roaring lion, looking for someone to devour." ~1 Peter 5:8 (NLT)

Junk can really get to us sometimes. It may be in the form of words. It may be in the form of thoughts. But Jesus never meant for us to collect junk. He came so that we may have abundant life (John 10:10b). He doesn't want us to be burdened down with so much junk that we can't function. And as long as we listen to the negative, we collect an abundance of junk in our trunks.

"And now, dear brothers and sisters, one final thing. Fix your thoughts on what is true, and honorable, and right, and pure, and lovely, and admirable. Think about things that are excellent and worthy of praise." ~Philippians 4:8 (NLT)

In order to get rid of the junk in our trunks, we have to begin to focus on the true, honorable, right, pure, lovely and admirable things. Focus on Jesus. When we start to do that, our lives will begin to get better and better.

"Seek the Kingdom of God above all else, and live righteously, and he will give you everything you need." ~Matthew 6:33 (NLT)

On a clear night in May 2012, God healed me of the junk in my trunk. Of course, it's an ongoing battle to keep the junk out. But let me tell you something, putting my focus on Jesus sure helps keep the junk at bay. And in the process I'm able to give others the reassurance that they too can get rid of their junk. There is hope, and a way out.

# Comfort Training
**October 25**

There are many hurting people in this world. Many of them don't even know they are hurting. They just know that something is wrong in their lives and they don't know how to fix it. That was me. For years I suffered periodic bouts of depression, anxiety, and feelings of such low self-esteem that I honestly believed that I must have done something to cause this to happen to me. I mean, that's what I was always told. Hearing "You brought this on yourself," repeatedly over the years, one begins to believe it truly is your fault that you are this way.

But I didn't bring it on myself. It wasn't my fault. And it's not yours, either. The various people in my life who had always blamed me for my emotional issues are the very people who had kept me in the state I was in; At least until I was healed. Because that was the night that the Lord reached down and said, "Enough!"

"[God] comforts us in all our troubles so that we can comfort others. When they are troubled, we will be able to give them the same comfort God has given us."
~2 Corinthians 1:4 (NLT, brackets mine)

Little did I know back then that the comfort God was giving me was to be distributed, by me, to others. At least, I didn't know *how* I was going to do it. I also didn't know to what degree I would be giving comfort. I just knew that I would, and that I needed to be ready and available.

I have spoken with many people. I have told my story. And I have had many women come to me and say, "When you were speaking, I was certain that you were telling my story!" How ironic that the things we have been through ran parallel to one another. That's how God works.

He takes each of us on a journey. Then, He gives each one of us a story to tell. A story that will in some way, help someone else. Just as the verse above says, God comforts us so we can comfort others in the same way. Someone, somewhere, is going through the same thing you've been through. And someday God will set up a Divine Appointment for you to meet, so you can comfort and encourage that person.

"...And you will be my witnesses in Jerusalem, and in all Judea and Samaria, and to the ends of the earth."
~Acts 1:8(b) (NIV)

Until that time, He is working on you, preparing you, training you, and getting you ready for your Appointment. I never realized that through all those years, I was being trained for this moment. I was getting my "Comfort Training." Not to bring attention to myself, but to testify to what God has done for me. For those little moments when I share my story and then someone comes to me and says, "Thank you for sharing what you've been through. It really encouraged me."

Never underestimate God or how far He will go to reach someone.

Here I am Lord... send me!

# Trust Issues
**December 18**

I've been broken and bruised both mentally, emotionally, physically, and spiritually. And while I talk about it, I don't do it to rehash the things I've been through, but to extend hope and healing to those of you who suffer the same things. You see, though I've been broken, I've been healed. Though some of those scars still remain in the healing process, the worst of it is gone. God healed me. Yet, being the human that I am, I remember. I remember because that's how humans are. So I'm using what I remember to bring glory to God. I'm using what I remember to help someone else who is stuck in the rut of oppression.

It's not easy being the recipient of yelling, screaming, or verbal, mental, or physical abuse. It's not easy to get over, either. But the good news about it is that, while God knows every single event of your life, He knows every single tear you have shed. He also knows the way out and will use every negative thing in your life to make something good out of it.

"We know that all things work together for the good of those who love God: those who are called according to His purpose." ~Romans 8:28 (HCSB)

You may be stuck in that rut today. May I encourage you? You won't be there for long. It might seem like a lifetime to you, but trust me it is but a moment to God. He is working something wonderful for you. It's up to you to hang in there and trust Him. It sure helps if you cry out to Him. He's there, listening, watching, and waiting.

Many years ago, I was at a youth camp with my oldest daughter. One day, as the adults went out for their activities, we were blindfolded then put into a line holding hands. There were about thirty of us. Then we were directed to walk through the woods, blindfolded, following the sound of the voice of the leader. We did as we were told and before long we came to a rope stretched across the trees. We were then told to find our way out of the woods, and our leader went silent. Following the rope, we walked, still blindfolded. But just as we thought we were to the end, we ran into other people, also blindfolded. We were at an impasse. What to do? It didn't take long before we discovered that there was another rope away from our designated rope. But we were instructed to stay together. We couldn't leave anyone. We worked and worked and before long, we found our way out and were told to remove our blindfolds. What did we learn? How to work together. But here's the real moral of the story: In order to get out of our dilemma, all we had to do was *ask*. If we had only called out to our leader, she would have come, taken us by the hand, and got us out of our mess. Uh-oh.

It's the same way with God. When we are in a mess, all we have to do is ask. Call out to Him and He is there, ready to help us out of any and every situation we are in. The only problem is we never think to ask. We are such a "Do-It-Yourself" bunch of people we think we can get ourselves out of our own messes. "You got yourself into that mess. Get yourself out!" is what we've grown up hearing. But it is such a lie directly from the father of lies, the devil. And the sad thing is we listen!

"When he [the devil] tells a lie, he speaks from his own nature, because he is a liar and the father of liars." ~John 8:44b (HCSB, brackets mine)

How do you think God feels when He watches us, His children, floundering around in our own pig sty of a mess, wishing we would only cry out to Him? Do you think He keeps us in the mess and doesn't come for help? He does come, in His timing. We may think He's left us to our own devices when in all actuality, He is teaching us a lesson. The lesson is different for each of us, but yet the same. The outcome may involve many different aspects, but one of them remains the same for us all; Trust in Him. Trust! Do we trust Him? We should.

"When I am afraid, I will trust in You. In God, whose word I praise, In God I trust; I will not fear. What can man do to me?" ~Psalm 56:3-4 (HCSB)

There are many things going on in the world today. Many people running this way and that, trying to figure out the meaning of life. There are many people trying to figure out the where's and why's of the things going on in the world. But if we would all just stop, and simply cry out to our Leader for help, He will. It's as simple as that. Just cry out to Jesus.

The best present you could ever receive is the forgiveness of Jesus Christ. But He won't force Himself on anyone. You have to come to Him and ask. I was in a bind for many, many years. I had no earthly idea that my issues could be resolved just by asking. I knew salvation. I knew prayer. I even knew to pray for others. But I did not know He would remove the deep-down-break-your-heart-I-have-lived-with-this-all-my-life issues, until one night when someone else called it out for me. That's when I knew. That's when He came. That's when I was healed.

Trust the Lord with everything you have. You won't regret it one bit. And I can tell you, it's the most wonderful experience you will ever have.

# Stepping Onto the Next Level

**December 30**

As one year left us... or maybe, as we left it behind and embraced the next, God brought me to a crossroads of sorts. Maybe He brought you to one as well. My particular crossroads, in all actuality was a staircase. There really wasn't a "take this road or this one" kind of situation for me. The path I'm on basically stayed the same, but there was another level that I had to get to. And the new year was time for me to climb. So I could either stay at the foot of the staircase and meander at the bottom throughout the new year, or I could begin my climb to the next level, where the Lord was trying to get me to go.

Sounds a little scary, doesn't it? What exactly does that mean? What is "the next level" anyway? I had no idea! I wouldn't know until I climbed the stairs. But here's the situation: it was my decision on whether I climb to the next level or not. The fact of the matter is, if I stayed where I was, I would still be where God had led me, but I wouldn't ever advance. If I climbed the stairs to the next level, "great and mighty things which [I] do not know" awaited me (Jeremiah 33:3). Now, that's where it gets exciting to me. For once in my life, I was not scared. I was truly excited! I didn't know what was at the top of the stairs, but I absolutely knew that God was standing just behind me with His hand on my back, steering me towards those stairs.

And here is yet another twist in this journey: the closer I

got to the stairs, the more slippery, bumpy, and gnarly the path got. I slipped up. I tripped. I caught myself on many things I should not have said, thought, or done. I felt awful for messing up and wondered where exactly I lost my oomph. Back when God shook me up and gave me a new path to follow, I was gung-ho about where I was going. But do you want to know something? I am not perfect. If I didn't have mistakes I wouldn't learn anything. I am still learning, I am still growing and the last time I tripped, I bumped right into God. Then I realized that not only did I know that God wanted to move me to the next level, but the enemy knew too, and he didn't like it one little bit.

"The thief comes only to steal and kill and destroy." ~John 10:10(a) (NIV)

As I was getting ready for church one Sunday morning, I said a quick prayer asking God to forgive me, and to speak through the pastor and give me a message. Going to church expecting God to show up; don't you know that He does. My slipping, tripping, and bumping the last few steps to the staircase took me right to the base of the stairs. The message God gave me was, "Take the first step. Trust Me." Well okie dokie!

In 2013, my life would change drastically. I didn't know exactly what I would be doing, but I was confident that it would be a deeper step into this ministry He has called me into. Once I got over and through the intimidation and oppression I suffered for years. Once I got over trying to "read between the lines" every intimidating person was hinting at around me. Once I realized that my life was not determined by what others think of me, but by what God wants of me...I was now ready to take the steps to the next level.

I went into a "Sold Out Believer" mode of my walk with God. I was no longer tolerant of anything less than that. However, that didn't mean that I wouldn't like certain people, places, or things. It just meant that, for me, I wouldn't be subjecting myself to things that do not bring glory to Him. Nor would I, to the best of my ability, subject myself to people or things that will tempt me to slip up. I wouldn't be perfect, nor did I expect to be. But it was the fact that I set my mind to try. And that is all that God is really after; My desire to at least strive for what He wants me to do. In that, I believe was my map to succeed.

As I said good-bye to 2012, I can truly say that God brought me through it and was now leading me to a new level in 2013. I didn't know what was in store. But I knew it would be exciting. And it was!

Shelley Wilburn

# Perfectly, Powerfully, and Permanently
### January 18, 2013

When I set out to do my website and write about my journey to forgiveness I had no idea where God would lead me. But He is definitely doing that and I'm following along. Sometimes reluctantly.

When I started this journey, I was newly healed from almost forty-seven years of mental and emotional abuse from various sources. Being healed of mental and emotional scars is quite a release of many things. But the most difficult part of it for me has been trust issues. I have had to learn to trust God more, lean on Him more and I have also had to learn how to be bold in talking to Him. Because growing up in a home where one is yelled at a lot, I had transferred that to God as well, thinking that if I talked to Him about my innermost fears, concerns, and such, He would get mad at me and yell at me. I was truly misguided.

I was watching a video in a marriage apps class at church, and in the first session I learned something very important. God loves me perfectly, powerfully, and permanently. He will never turn His back on me. He will never get mad at me. He will never leave me (Hebrews 5). He has promised this. I knew this in my head but since, have learned it in my heart.

In my friendships, I had transferred my feelings to my friends. But they couldn't give me what I needed. In reality, they often made things worse. They didn't know that deep inside me, I was just longing for someone to trust. But people will let you down, just as I let them down.

In my marriage, I realized that I had also transferred my feelings to my husband, and was trusting him to give me what I needed, which he can't. Nor can I give him what he needs. I was using what I saw in my parents and grandparents to base my feelings on that I had for my husband. This was and is a very bad idea. I had no earthly idea that in order to have the kind of relationship with my husband I was supposed to have I needed to put my focus on Christ. For years, I struggled with this, fearing if I did that then my husband would get mad at me. Little did I know that he was desiring the same thing. We can't depend solely on ourselves or our spouses (or others) to fill what only God can.

God's love in us produces the fruit of the Spirit, making us capable to love and receive love (Galatians 5:16-25). It is a must to stay connected to Him in prayer, fellowship, and His Word.

"But the Holy Spirit produces this kind of fruit in our lives: love, joy, peace, patience, kindness, goodness, faithfulness, gentleness, and self-control." ~Galatians 5:22-23(a) (NLT)

Something else that I have learned is that listening to the advice of others will only cause more problems in my marriage. For years I allowed the controlling, oppressiveness of parents, grandparents, and often others in my life to dictate what I did and how I felt. Wrong ideas create wrong mindsets. The very thing I sought was the very thing they ridiculed. But thank God He healed me of these wrong mindsets and set me back on the path I'm supposed to be on!

Matthew 6 talks about wherever your treasure is there your heart will be also. Where was my treasure all these years? It was wadded up in the misconception that someone needed to serve me. Here's a little secret for you: Trust God, not your feelings. Because feelings can be fickle, and the enemy will twist and turn them to manipulate you into believing that you need people, places, money, etc. in order to be happy, when all you really need is Jesus. Every time we turn to God He fills us with His supernatural love. When you do that you won't have to rely on the advice of others to figure out what it is you need out of life. You'll already have it. Perfectly, powerfully and permanently.

# Setbacks, Struggles, and Stress
**January 22**

I had a minor setback one morning. It didn't feel like a setback in the beginning, though. What it felt like to me, was the beginning of a heart attack. Trust me when I say that I was a bit concerned. Okay, not concerned as much as a little scared. Okay, not a little scared...a lot scared!

Heart disease runs in my family. But let me explain something. So does cancer, arthritis, high blood pressure, diabetes, depression, anxiety, oppression, the need to control, and many other things. But I had decided I was going to rise above it. I was not going to follow in my family's footsteps and let these things dictate my life and how it would play out and ultimately end. No sir!

I had decided that Jesus was going to rule my life. I decided that He was in charge and through Him I can do all things, because He gives me the strength to do so (Philippians 4:13). However, I began to get a little comfortable in my new walk, my new healing, that I became a little too confident and let my guard down for just a bit...and I had a setback.

I realize that I will have ups and downs, just like everybody else. But what I hadn't counted on was it sneaking up on me. I don't know why I didn't think of that, because 1 Peter 5:8 warns, "Be sober, be vigilant, because your adversary the devil, walks about like a roaring lion, seeking whom he may devour" (NKJV). And when I say he's sneaky, that's quite an understatement. Because he will lie in wait until I have forgotten to set my guard. He will wait until I'm not paying attention, or putting off my prayer time, or my Bible reading time, and then he will attack.

This particular morning, he attacked by giving me chest pain. I've had them before because I have a hiatal hernia that sometimes flares up and causes these pains, in the exact spot I was having them this particular morning, and in just the same way I have always had them but since I had not had them in many months, I had forgotten. I wasn't prepared. Therefore I thought I was in the beginnings of a heart attack. So I did what every normal housewife does when in distress: I called my husband.

My Grandma Ann used to tell me (repeatedly), "You've got such a good husband." She was right. He came rushing home to check on me. When he walked in the door, I started crying. Then he reminded me of some things that had happened in the past twenty-four hours, and the light bulb came on. You see, as soon as I realized my mistake, the pains left. As soon as I realized what I had been going through, and then when the pains hit, I knew. I had been duped by the enemy. Oh, *maaan*!

But here's the best part about it. Even though I still had a slight twinge of pain (more a nuisance than anything), I realized that I had not had my prayer time. So, I went. While it was just a short prayer time, I denounced the pain. I thanked the Lord for His love and for His always being there. And I apologized for my negligence. Oh yes, He can and still will use me. His Word promises that. But my minor setback only proved to strengthen my resolve to pay more attention and to focus even more on the Lord.

"If we confess our sins, He is faithful and just to forgive us our sins and to cleanse us from all unrighteousness." ~1 John 1:9 (NKJV)

You see, stress and the Holy Spirit don't mix. In fact, the Holy Spirit knocks stress right out the door. I have but to think the thought, and He comes running in and takes care of things. I had not been under any stress at all for months. Not like I was having this morning. But one evening, I had a visit from a family member who was struggling with some issues. As we talked, as I listened and gave comfort and encouragement, I forgot to pay attention to the fact that for this reason, I keep my distance from family. The oppression, the need to control the lives of others, the lack of encouragement and support, the constant throwing the past back at you, and the constant feeling that you aren't good enough for anything, is what God healed me of many months ago. I had not dealt with any of that in so long that I had forgotten what if felt like, until this one morning.

The weight of oppression was so strong that it literally gave me chest pains. But through Christ, His mercy, and His grace, the Holy Spirit took care of it. It was like recharging my spiritual batteries. Oh how my heart hurts for those suffering under the weight of oppressing and intimidating people. I lived it for years. And when I married out from under it, the mental and emotional scars that it left kept me in a continual state of oppression and kept me under the control of the very people I married out from under. Nearly forty-seven years of being controlled by various people, being manipulated by others, being intimidated by others, suffering depression, panic, anxiety, feelings of unworthiness, loneliness, despair, rejection, and ultimately thoughts of suicide—all these things were swept out of my life with one touch, one breath, from God.

People want to know why I write the things I do. This is why: the fact that I was healed of it; the fact that I struggle every day with keeping Christ first in my life. The fact that I know there are others out there who are suffering needlessly. If my story helps just one, then I did my job and it was well worth it.

I can't just walk up to someone and say, "Hey, I know what your problem is and if you'll let Jesus heal you, your life will be so much better." One, they'll think I'm crazy, and two, they'll tell me it's none of my business. But, by writing about my own experiences, opens up my life to others and lets them see that yes, I have been there, I have suffered, and I know exactly what they are going through. I lived it and I survived!

I'm a survivor. You are, too. Don't let the enemy rule over you anymore. Don't let him use others to control and manipulate and intimidate you. You have power over this. If you know Jesus, then you have all the power you need to stomp the enemy and his games. Use it. Use your Trump Card. If you need reinforcements, contact me. I'll be happy to pray for you, declaring victory over you, in the name of Jesus. Because if you read the back of the Rule Book (the Bible), we win!

"The God of peace will soon crush Satan under your feet. The grace of our Lord Jesus be with you." ~Romans 16:20 (NLT)

# Moving On!
**February 2**

Onward and upward! There is only so much you can do before you have to move on. For years I stayed in a constant state of oppression for which I was miserable. But one day I decided that I was sick of my mental and emotional state. I was tired of living day to day being knocked down by the words and insensitivity of others. I was tired of living by what others thought of me and what others tried to tell me to do.

Here I was, a forty-six-year-old mother-of-three, Nonney-to-two (at the time), wife-of-one who couldn't function throughout the day without her mind wandering and replaying hurtful things people said to me over, and over, and over, and over.

I knew Jesus. I served Him (I thought). And I knew that there had to be more to life than what I was living, but I didn't know how to access it, or get to it. One thing I did know, there was something going on at the church I was attending and by golly I wanted some of it. No, I wanted a whole bunch of it. I wanted my mind healed. I wanted out of this crazy, mixed-up, broken record of a mental state that I was in. It was time for me to move on. I got that on May 30, 2012.

I talk about that date a lot and I will repeat that a lot, because that date is very significant in my life. It was a turning point for me. It was a day well, night that God healed my mind and turned my life around. And while I started a website to write about my story, it isn't finished yet. It won't be finished until I step into eternity. I hope that won't be for a long, long time. I would like to be like author Mary Higgins Clark; in my eighties and still writing strong! That though, will be according to God's plan for me.

But as I write about the things that God has healed me of, I also realize I must move even from that. There is so much more to this journey than where I have come from. There is more to where I am going. There is more to what I am learning. And to you who are reading, there is also hope.

I came from a place in my life where I was ready to give up hope. I thought I was destined to live in this "hell hole" of mental destruction for the rest of my life, and to die a miserable, lonely, bitter, old woman. My maternal grandmother died like that. I never wanted it.

My hope came rushing in on that clear, May night. I was given a new outlook on life. I was given a new mental state. I was given a new everything from the inside out and I was joyous. I was given a story to tell. There are people out there who are suffering as I did who need to know that there is hope for them, too. You can get out of that mental state you are in. You can survive. The enemy wants to keep you down, but God wants to raise you up.

It's time to move on. It's time to move up. It's time to put your shoes on and let God lead you into something wonderful. It may sound crazy, but if you are in the trenches and can't find your way out, let me tell you right now, grab onto the rope. You might be saying right now, "I don't know how!" I didn't know how, either. But someone led me out, and I want to lead you out. Trust me. Jesus is the only way to get out of where you're at. But you have to trust Him.

"Jesus told him, "I am the way, the truth, and the life. No one can come to the Father except through me." ~John 14:6 (NLT)

Now that I'm out, I discovered that there is even more than I realized. And since I have been writing, there is even more than that. It is time for me to move on and move up. Won't you join me?

# Can't Keep Me Down!
**February 7**

For years, I was knocked down by the words and actions of others. I learned how to read signs and body language so I would know how to defend myself. I was broken, battered, and bruised, but God would not let me be kept down.

"My defense and shield depend on God, Who saves the upright in heart." ~Psalm 7:10 (Amplified Bible)

Jesus was knocked down, too. He was beaten, battered, and bruised. He was ridiculed, spat upon, tested, and people talked behind His back. Then ultimately, He was killed. But God would not let Him be kept down, either. Because three days later, Jesus rose from the dead proving that you can't keep a Good Man down!

Because of what Jesus did on the cross, He made a way for me and for you to be able to get back up when the chips are down. We don't have to be held captive by words, actions, neglect, intimidation, oppression, or any other negative thing that lurks in the shadows, seeking to destroy us.

When God healed me, He gave me a new heart, a new outlook on life, a new purpose, and He pointed me in the direction He wanted me to go. I felt as if I were being told, "They can't keep a good girl down. Now, go out there and show 'em what I've taught you!"

"The Lord preserves the simple; I was brought low, and He saved me." ~Psalm 116:6 (NKJV)

When someone asks me, "Who is Jesus to you?" I smile and immediately say, "Healer!" Of course, Jesus is so much more to me than that. Ultimately, He is my Healer, because without the healing my story, my website, even this book would not be here. I could not do what I'm doing now if it weren't for Him healing me. He is my everything but He is also my Healer.

I want Him to be your everything and your Healer, too. There isn't anything you're going through, or have gone through, that He can't fix. You aren't too far away. You haven't done something so terrible that He won't accept you. Don't listen to the lies of the enemy anymore. Instead, prove to him and everyone else that he can't keep a good woman, or man, down! Prove it to them all! Step out and say, "God, I need to be fixed!" Ask Him to help you, to heal you. Then give it all to Him. Turn it loose. Let it fly like a helium balloon.

"And now, Lord, what do I wait for and expect? My hope and expectation are in You." ~Psalm 39:7 (Amplified Bible)

The next time someone tries to put you down, smile, and remember that God won't let you be kept down.

# Where Do I Fit In?!
**February 11**

Many people point and laugh at times, because I wear mismatched socks. Yes, I have matching socks. I choose to mismatch them. "Why?" is the next question they ask me. "Why do you wear mismatched socks?" There is a reason for it. No, I'm not trying to get attention, or to be silly. I'm not even trying to make a statement, although wearing the mismatched socks has in fact made one.

    I started wearing mismatched socks because of a little joke I made in my "About Me" post on my website, stating that I liked to wear them. After I posted it, I began thinking about them more and more. The thing is, I made a lot of silly statements in that post, just because I wanted to make people laugh, and wanted them to know that I was lighthearted and liked to have fun. But having posted things like the fact that I like candy and my family says I like Halloween because I can "legally" ride a broom (not so), those things didn't remain in my thoughts like mismatched socks did.

    I began to see mismatched socks in a people perspective. I was talking to a friend of mine about my website and mentioned the mismatched socks. The next statement sealed the fate of them: "Mismatched socks, though they don't match, are still useful, like people. I don't fit in with things other people do. I am a mismatched sock! But God plucked me out of the laundry basket of life and said, "I can still use her." My friend looked at me and I could see understanding dawn on her. She began to smile and then said, "I totally understand that!"

I know many people out there who are suffering many different things. You wonder where you fit in. Whether you struggle with physical, mental, or emotional abuse, depression, feelings of hopelessness, or whatever drags you down, God wants to lift you back up. He wants to pluck you out of the laundry basket of life, too. He can still use you. There *is* something He wants you to do. There *is* someplace where you fit in.

When I look down and see my mismatched pair of socks, I am reminded of the healing God did on me. I am reminded that all the things of my past are forgiven and forgotten. I am reminded that God gave me a task to tell my story so that someone else out there can be encouraged and given hope. He placed me where I fit in. Whether that's you, or someone you know, is beside the point. The point of the matter is *you* matter!

God loves you so much and He has a place where you fit in. All you have to do is ask Him to show you.

# Short-Circuited

**February 26**

When I was fifteen years old, I slipped into a severe state of depression. It felt as if a giant boulder came and deposited itself on my chest and shoulders. Feelings of despair, hopelessness, fear—no, terror, and many negative things crept into my mind. I literally felt as if the world was going to come to an end and I was going to be left behind. I have absolutely no idea why I felt like that.

The reason I can remember it is because I dealt with it, alone, for many years. Because when I slipped into it, I got no help at all. There was no medical help for me. I was never taken to the doctor. I was told that I would be committed to a mental institution if the doctor found out. I was told the only person who could help me was me. I was yelled at to straighten up. Then ultimately the inevitable happened; my situation, I was told, was my fault. I was told I brought it all on myself.

I tried to pray. I tried to trust Jesus. But it just wasn't working. I was short-circuited. How, you might ask? Unbelief. Even after I had asked Jesus into my heart, had trusted Him as my Lord and Savior, some things just didn't work for me. The main two were my continual spiral into depression and my struggle with my weight. I had a short in the circuitry of my faith that was preventing the Lord from helping me. It prevented Him from working His miracles in me.

I was watching a sermon by Creflo Dollar and it struck me when he said, "When your faith is not working, there is unbelief present somewhere." Ouch! I realized that my entire life seemed to have short-circuited my belief.

It took literally thirty years to finally splice my circuits together to see results. That is a very long time to deal with mental and emotional issues. But I honestly didn't know that it was unbelief that was preventing me from having the life God intended for me to have. Not that I didn't believe in Jesus. But I had this little doubt that He could help me with my mind. Remember, I was always told it was my fault. I literally had to have intervention by people whom the Lord had prepared to intervene for me. Because of their faith, they helped me to have faith and to believe that maybe, just maybe, God could heal me. And He did!

"…This faith was given to you because of the justice and fairness of Jesus Christ, our God and Savior."
~2 Peter 1:1(b) NLT

After God healed my mind and healed me from the years of mental and emotional intimidation and oppression, I began to grow and learn. It was as if a veil had been lifted and I was stepping into a brand new me. The first time I came under spiritual attack after that healing, I could feel my faith kick into gear. I knew I was being attacked spiritually. But I could also feel it being deflected off my faith. There was a shield over my heart and the attacks were literally bouncing off that shield. God gave me a physical demonstration of how He was helping me overcome the very things I used to allow to control me. That, in turn, helped build my faith even more.

# My Chains Are Gone!
**March 12**

"I just feel like someone needs to hear this. If God has healed you of something, your chains are broken. You need to know that they truly are broken and you truly are free. So shake off your chains and move forward!"

The man who spoke these words one night at church did not know why he was supposed to say them, but I did. I'm sure there were others who needed them as well, but at that moment, it was just God and me.

Have you ever had a moment when you thought all your hard work was for naught? I have prayed for something before only to have the situation get worse before it gets better. Why is that? Because the enemy knows that when we go boldly to the throne room of grace, amazing things happen.

"So if the Son liberates you [makes you free men], then you are really and unquestionably free."
~John 8:36 (Amplified Bible)

My healing came and my life changed. My chains were broken. My chains were gone. Things started to get better. They got so much better that they began to get worse. Why? Because, I was finally able to stand for what I believed in and not back down because of intimidation. I was finally able to talk about the things that kept me hiding in the pit of depression. I was beginning to tell others about the hope I had, and that they can have in trusting Jesus and the enemy got threatened by it. So he began to throw darts at me.

At first the darts just bounced off. And don't you know that if an enemy attacks and doesn't succeed, they are going to come back with bigger and better fighting power. This last round of fighting power caused me to stumble. But hang on just a minute. I may stumble, but even if I fall, I still come out the winner. So do you.

We often get sidetracked by enemy attack. It may not seem like an enemy attack at first. At first it may seem like a friend has turned her back on you for no reason. It may seem like family has shunned you. You may feel like everyone around you is running you into the ground. Yes, it's hurtful, but remember that Jesus went through the same things. He understands. And He has provided for you a safe tower to run to; Him.

"The name of the Lord is a strong tower; the [consistently] righteous man [upright and in right standing with God] runs into it and is safe, high [above evil] and strong."
~Proverbs 18:10 (Amplified Bible)

"For You have been a shelter and a refuge for me, a strong tower against the adversary." ~Psalm 61:3 (Amplified Bible)

Yes, things are changing. Is that really so awful bad? If you think about it these things are just temporary. And the changes that are happening could just prove to be God rearranging your life so that He can do something wonderfully amazing. Your chains have been broken. Sweep the pieces up and throw them in the trash where they belong. Then watch and listen because I believe God is getting ready to do something powerful. You don't want to miss it.

# You Are On Purpose
**March 25**

You are chosen... You are anointed... You are gifted... You have what it takes... You have been appointed...

As I listened to these words during a sermon at church, it began to occur to me that these words were not only for the people around me, but they were actually for *me*. *I* am chosen... *I* am anointed... *I* am gifted... *I* have what it takes... and *I* have been appointed! Me! Appointed!

The night God healed me of all the mental and emotional garbage I carried around for years, He also supplied me with a key Bible verse to go with it. When I read it, it encouraged me and reminded me of the very fact that I have indeed been chosen, anointed, and gifted to do what I do. It is mentioned in two separate places, and it also applies to Jesus. However, when I read it, I truly felt the Lord saying, "I'm giving this to you, too. Now go out and do what you've been chosen to do." What an honor.

**Old Testament:**
"The Spirit of the Sovereign Lord is upon me, for the Lord has anointed me to bring good news to the poor. He has sent me to comfort the brokenhearted and to proclaim that captives will be released and prisoners will be freed. He has sent me to tell those who mourn that the time of the Lord's favor has come, and with it, the day of God's anger against

their enemies." ~Isaiah 61:1-2 (NLT)

**New Testament:**
"The Spirit of the Lord is upon me, for he has anointed me to bring Good News to the poor. He has sent me to proclaim that captives will be released, that the blind will see, that the oppressed will be set free, and that the time of the Lord's favor has come." ~Luke 4:18-19 (NLT)

When Jesus came, these Scriptures were fulfilled. When He healed my mind and emotions, He placed this in me and sent me out to tell my story of healing so that I in turn, could help someone else who is going through the turmoil of mental and emotional intimidation by others.

The Lord does not want you to live in distress. He also doesn't want you to live under the hand of oppression or intimidation. When He heals you, He sets you apart, anoints you, and gives you your purpose. He had plans for you even before the day you were conceived. You are not an accident. You are on purpose. You are most definitely the masterpiece that God has chosen to do what it is that He has placed in you to do.

What has the Lord placed in your heart to do? What burns within you to be released? Take it to the Lord and give Him everything in you then watch and see where He takes you, because you are not a mistake. You are on purpose!

Shelley Wilburn

# Answer the Phone
**April 10**

Hey! Answer your phone! No, not your cell phone. No, not your land line either, if you even still have one of those. You need to answer your spiritual phone.

You have a calling on your life. You have a purpose. Your age doesn't matter. Your physical abilities do not matter. All that matters is your salvation. You've been saved? And you are still breathing? Then you most definitely have a calling. You have a ministry. Oh yes, you do! Yet, you still think God can't use you?

"I knew you before I formed you in your mother's womb. Before you were born I set you apart and appointed you as my prophet to the nations." ~Jeremiah 1:5 (NLT)

Before you were even thought of, God was programming you for some sort of ministry. You have it in you already. All you have to do is use it. Sure, I used to think that God couldn't use me. I mean, I didn't have a huge testimony. There was not any "lightning bolt" type of crash and the Hallelujah Chorus start playing. Mine was subtle but it was there nonetheless. So is yours.

My ministry came after a thirty-some-odd-year hiatus. The reason for the lapse is because I was literally consumed in a well of intimidation so deep that I didn't even recognize it. But thank God that someone else did! That Someone was Jesus, and He sent others to help rescue me out of the pit of darkness that held me frozen in intimidation.

When God healed me of that, I could hear the spiritual phone inside me ringing. I answered it and you are now reading my ministry. My passion is writing. God placed in my heart a desire to write my experiences; to write something so unique that people read it and go, "Yeah! I get that! It sounds like my life, too! Wow, I'm not the only one!" But don't misunderstand; I don't do this to impress you. I do this to serve God. He is the One who is speaking to you through me.

What is He saying to you? What is it that burns within you? What are you passionate about? Let me encourage you today. If you have been saved then you are most definitely called to minister in some way, shape, or form. Maybe not behind a pulpit. Maybe not oversees as a missionary. But you are definitely called!

"A spiritual gift is given to each of us so we can help each other. To one person the Spirit gives the ability to give wise advice; to another the same Spirit gives a message of special knowledge..." ~1 Corinthians 12:7-8 NLT (also see verses 9-11)

You have a very special gift. God wants you to use it to help someone, or several someones. My gift is right here, giving encouragement to those of you who are suffering intimidation, oppression, depression, and whatever else it is that keeps you tied down.

It's time to answer the phone. Why not pick up and ask

Shelley Wilburn

God what it is that He wants you to do?

# Ch-Ch-Ch-Changes
**April 17**

Change is in the air! At least it is around my house. There are a lot of things going on and not just around here, but all over the USA and the world. And while there are a lot of negative things going on, one thing remains the same—Jesus! He never changes.

"Jesus Christ is the same yesterday, today, and forever."
~Hebrews 13:8 (NLT)

I'll admit we are creatures of habit. We get in a rut and before long we are doing the same thing different day and we become so set in our ways that change becomes a four-letter-word. We don't want to try new things. We don't want to visit new places. But the crazy thing is, if we don't make changes we won't grow. Whether physically, mentally, emotionally, or even spiritually, change is quite often a good thing, if it helps you to move forward into the place that God has prepared for you.

"As Christians we should never fear change. We must believe in change so long as it is change oriented toward godliness. The Christian life is a life of continual change."
~Jay Adams, *Godliness Through Discipline* (1972)

I had just such a change. Yes, I was fearful. But at the

same time, I was ready. I was so tired of the way things were going. I was so beaten down mentally and emotionally. I tried to stay upbeat and happy, but it's so difficult when you have no idea what it is that is causing you to feel this way.

It came to me one afternoon when I finally told D.A., "I want my mind healed." I knew enough to know that it was something from my past, something that had been drilled into me, said to me, continually pressed against me, that was keeping me the prisoner of my own mind. Joyce Meyer talks about this issue in her book, *Battlefield of the Mind*. This is where I began to see how thoughts, words, and situations can dominate our minds and cause us a world of problems like anxiety, stress, feelings of worthlessness, anger, bitterness, etc. Reading Joyce's book and teaching series were paramount in turning me onto the path of eventual healing. But I had to get to the point where I was ready.

Until you are ready, you will never change. Until you are ready, you will not seek out the healing that God has waiting for you. On May 30, 2012, I was ready, and I knew that something was going to change that night.

"He will take our weak mortal bodies and change them into glorious bodies like his own, using the same power with which he will bring everything under his control."
~Philippians 3:21 (NLT)

Sure enough, it did! With the prayers of godly people surrounding me, and a spiritual coach leading me, God healed my mind and introduced me to my new Best Friend, the Holy Spirit. Together, we began a journey that is still going on today. Every day is something new. Every day something changes. While the world spins out of control, it really isn't out of control. God knows exactly what's going on and He is watching. He is taking care of those who trust in Him.

We may not understand change. We may not understand why bad things happen to good people, to innocent people. But no matter what, we can trust and believe that God is in control of all of it. Our job is to trust Him, to confide in Him, and to rest in Him. Changes come. If we are focused on the Lord, those changes won't be so big after all.

Shelley Wilburn

# Leave Your Light On
**April 26**

The lights are on, but nobody's home! I have heard that statement many times throughout the years. That statement was made as a joke, usually about me, by various people in my life. And they always laughed. But I didn't.

We are often made fun of because of our looks, our actions, our beliefs, and many other things that others don't understand. It's called persecution. And as a Christ follower, we endure it even harder at times. The outside world tries to put out our light, whether physically, mentally emotionally, or spiritually. But we are told that our light should shine for everyone to see.

"You are the light of the world—like a city on a hilltop that cannot be hidden... let your good deeds shine out for all to see, so that everyone will praise your heavenly Father." ~Matthew 5:14, 16(b) (NLT)

Many times we think we have to stand and fight, when all we really have to do is just stand and shine. I used to think I had to have a snappy comeback for every person who attacked me. Whether it was an insult, a nasty joke, or just an outright attack, I would usually feel the burn from my head to my toes and end up lashing out. That's about the time that my attacker would begin laughing sarcastically in my face. I could literally see in their eyes the crazed, lunatic-like enjoyment that they were getting, knowing that I just messed up.

All that mattered to them now was that I made a mistake. They saw my light and quickly tried to extinguish it. And I allowed them to cause it to dim. But now, I have learned to stand.

"Therefore take up the whole armor of God that you may be able to withstand in the evil day, and having done all, to stand." ~Ephesians 6:13 (NKJV)

My lights are always on, yet I don't always answer the door. I let faith go instead. I have learned that I don't have to fight like I used to. I never had to. In the past though, because of the constant intimidation and manipulation, I was always on the defensive. But when God healed me, He replaced the intimidation and oppression with peace and a confidence so strong that, when faced with those who thought they could still intimidate me, I stayed calm, quiet, and just looked at them.

The enemy saw my lights on. He sent intimidation to knock at my door, but I didn't answer. And my would-be intimidator was at a loss for words or actions. This is what happens when we use the Word of God to stand on instead of the standards of the world.

"So humble yourselves before God. Resist the devil, and he will flee from you." ~James 4:7 (NLT)

Don't be intimidated when trials comes knocking. They

will definitely come. But how we handle them will mean the difference between letting our light shine or causing it to dim. Be strong in the Lord, leave your lights on, stand and let faith answer the door.

# Put Your Foot Down
**May 9**

I think it's time to put your foot down. It's time to put your foot on the neck of your enemies and take authority over the things that are controlling you. It may sound a little harsh...to put your foot on the neck of your enemies. But if you have lived under intimidation, manipulation, control of any kind, then you know what I'm talking about.

In the spiritual world Christians wrestle every day with forces that try their best to intimidate us, manipulate us, and control us. The very things that make us cringe are the things that the enemy (Satan) will use against us to prevent us from growing and living the abundant life that Christ died in order for us to have. Satan will even use people in his employ to do it to us.

"For we are not fighting against flesh-and-blood enemies, but against evil rulers and authorities of the unseen world, against mighty powers in this dark world, and against evil spirits in the heavenly places." ~Ephesians 6:12 (NLT)

For years I lived in fear of what others thought about me. Having been raised being scrutinized, judged, manipulated and intimidated, I feared what people would do if I stepped one toe out of line (their specifications, not mine). I hated confrontation because it usually meant that someone didn't like something that I said or did. In the past,

I had many people who didn't like the things I did and let me know about it, whether it was how I dressed, how I looked, what I weighed, all the way to how I kept my house, raised my kids, or even how often I went to church and where. The words spoken to me throughout the years were hurtful to me because they came from people I loved, therefore those words stuck with me creating a type of bondage making me afraid to physically do anything.

These things created many strongholds within me such as fear of what someone might say, remembered insults and verbal attacks and the like. Those were the things that controlled me when I was alone, keeping me from functioning. I became the victim of my own mind, allowing anxiety, worry, depression, panic, and imagined conversations to control every move I made. When I was around actual people I could not function properly. Certain people knew how to control me whether it was a derogatory comment, presented as a joke, or a direct insult or confrontation. I allowed it for too many years.

When God healed my mind, He also sent me on a journey to learn exactly how to put my foot on the neck of my enemies and take back the life He gave me. The term to "put your foot on the neck of your enemy" is to take authority. We have been given the authority by Jesus Christ, to take charge of our situations. We do not have to let others control or intimidate us. We do not have to suffer depression, intimidation, manipulation, or any other mind game the enemy throws at us.

There are many places in the Bible where people overcame their enemies simply by obeying what God told them to do. They received His favor over their lives, and He took care of them. In the Book of Joshua, there were five evil kings who had heard of Joshua's victory over the enemies of the children of Israel. These kings banded together to overtake Joshua and destroy him, but God had other plans. He delivered these kings and all the people of the land into the hands of the children of Israel.

When Joshua captured the five kings, he didn't immediately kill them. Since God had delivered their enemies into their hands, they would not be defeated but their enemies would. Joshua could have killed the kings himself, but look how he encouraged the Israelites and taught them that they too had the authority over their enemies:

"Joshua told the commanders of his army, "Come and put your feet on the kings' necks." And they did as they were told. "Don't ever be afraid or discouraged," Joshua told his men. "Be strong and courageous, for the Lord is going to do this to all of your enemies." ~Joshua 10:24b-25 (NLT)

God has given us the same authority that He gave to Joshua and that He gave to the Israelites. We have the assurance of victory over our enemies and strongholds simply by trusting the Lord and taking authority over those things and people that bully us. When we stand up for what we know God has told us to do, nothing will touch us.

"Stand your ground, putting on the belt of truth and the body armor of God's righteousness." ~Ephesians 6:14 (NLT)

No more will depression, anxiety, worry, manipulation,

or intimidation bully me. Neither will someone who wants to stop me from what God has called me to do. I am putting my foot down and I'm keeping it down. I am not the same person I was last year, or even thirty years ago. One of the greatest moments since my healing was when my husband looked at me with surprise and stated, "People don't intimidate you anymore, do they!" My answer: "No."

It's time to take a stand. It's time to put your foot down. Take the authority that God has given to you. Say, "No more!" Stand. Then God will do the rest.

# I Am a Lazarus
**May 19**

He was dead for four days. I'm pretty sure he didn't smell very good, either. He just got sick one day and before his sisters knew it, he was gone. Their brother Lazarus was dead. They had sent for their good Friend, Jesus. But He didn't make it in time to save Lazarus. Or did He? Because, it really wasn't about Lazarus dying. It was about something a whole lot bigger.

"When Jesus heard it, He said, "This sickness will not end in death but is for the glory of God, so that the Son of God may be glorified through it." ~John 11:4 (HCSB)

So, Jesus waited a little longer before He went to check on Lazarus. By this time, Lazarus had been buried for four days and probably smelled worse than a polecat. Yet, Jesus yelled for him to come out and, miracle of miracles, Lazarus got up; *from the dead* (John 11:38-44). He became a walking, talking miracle. How many people can say that? Hang on just one second. Even today, there are many people who can say that. I know because I am one of them. I am a Lazarus; a walking, talking miracle.

For over forty years I was a mental and emotional "basket case" as some people would call me. My family drilled it in my head that I was destined to suffer depression because, "It runs in the family." They also told me that I was destined to be fat because, "It runs in the family." Then my own mother contracted cancer and died. I thought that too was my destiny because, "It runs in the family," even though I have always been very healthy and strong. Yet it was still spoken over me by surviving members of my family and others.

I read the Bible passages that stated that God had plans for me, that He wanted to prosper me, not harm me. He wanted to give me hope and a future (Jeremiah 29:11). I read where if I just believed, I would receive everything I asked for in prayer (Matthew 21:22). Promise after promise I read, but it never sank in because of the negative, hurtful things that had been spoken over me most of my life. Of course I would pray, but it was for little things and always for someone else because God just couldn't help me. He could save me so that when I did die I would go to heaven. But all those other things, well I just figured that they were for other people. Right? No.

Those things *are* for me, too. And just like He did to Lazarus, one night Jesus called me to "come out!" And I did! The mental and emotional baggage I carried were thrown into the fire. The worries about my appearance were thrown down. The worries of terminal illness were banished. Just like Lazarus, I was healed. And just like Lazarus, there have been those who do not appreciate what Jesus did for me.

It's really sad that when someone receives a miracle in their lives, others try to knock them back down. Yet it happens. People I have known for years still say, "I know you. I know how to get to you." I really don't know why they think they need to "get to me" but apparently they do. Bringing up my past though isn't going to diminish the fact that I am a walking, talking, writing miracle. Just like that of Lazarus.

Let me tell you something: God isn't concerned about what others say or think about you. He cares about *you*. Let me tell you that if you step out in faith, believing and receiving His grace, mercy, forgiveness, and healing, He will meet you at your decision, at your first step, and take care of you. Then you too, will be a Lazarus.

"Jesus said to her, "I am the resurrection and the life. The one who believes in Me, even if he dies, will live. Everyone who lives and believes in Me will never die, ever. Do you believe this?" ~John 11:25-26 (HCSB)

You don't have to listen to the enemy. You don't have to listen to those around you who speak lies and negative things. Instead, listen to Jesus. Believe in Him, trust Him, and wait on Him. When you do, amazing and miraculous things will happen. Because even when Jesus was four days late, He was right on time.

Shelley Wilburn

# A Year In My Life
**May 30**

As I looked back through my posts on my website, I saw so many changes, so much spiritual growth, and so many blessings. It was one year ago, May 30, 2013 that God healed my mind and my soul and placed me on this journey. What started out as a journey to forgiveness turned into so much more than that. It's not just about finding forgiveness for others, but finding mercy, grace, and especially hope in the struggles that we face daily and the people we come in contact with. It's about finding our purpose. But above all of that, this journey is about growing closer and closer in our relationship with Jesus. Because you see, without Him none of this would be possible.

One year earlier I made the decision that I wanted my mind healed of all the pent-up emotions that were keeping me prisoner of my own mind. I wanted healing from the intimidation and manipulation that I suffered at the hands of many. I wanted to grow in my spiritual walk. I wanted a close relationship and even closer one with Jesus, with my husband, with my kids and with my grandkids. I knew deep within my soul that I would never have that as long as I battled things in my mind.

With that decision, I had no earthly idea what was about to happen to me. I was a little hesitant, a little apprehensive about going forward at church and asking for someone to please pray with me for God to heal my mind. But here's where everything shifts into something totally amazing. God already knew my decision, knew my heart, and knew what I wanted and He already prepared everything and every person to be there when I stepped forward.

This is how awesome and amazing our God works. When my pastor met me at the front of the church, *he* told *me* what I was there for. When he prayed for me, when others prayed for me, they spoke the very things that I was afraid to speak and that I did not know how to speak. Yet, here they were, interceding on my behalf and here I was, agreeing with them repeating what they said, and telling God, "I receive that!" What happened next is nothing but a miracle.

God healed me from the bottoms of my feet to the top of my head. It's such an amazing thing to actually feel your soul heave a sigh of complete relief. How can I put this in terms others can understand; it was as if a giant eraser swiped through my mind and cleared away all the graffiti that had been marking up my thoughts and my view. All those recordings of the hurtful words people said to me were erased and I was free. For the first time in my life I was *free*. The next morning, God gave me Scripture to show me the path He had put me on.

"The Spirit of the Lord is on Me, because He has anointed Me to preach good news to the poor. He has sent Me to proclaim freedom to the captives and recovery of sight to the blind, to set free the oppressed, to proclaim the year of the Lord's favor." ~Luke 4:18-19 (HCSB)

I'm still free. Of course there are still battles within my mind, but I am now better equipped to handle them. I still have verbal abuse thrown my way, but I can bat it away much better. Those who want control can't have it. There is no room for them, only room for the Lord. He has shifted my entire existence. I am closer to Him, closer to my husband, my kids, and my grandkids now. I have new friends who spur me on, encourage me, and accept me for me. Do I miss my past? No. I miss what could have been if things were different. But I can't dwell on that. Those who are in my past, even though I love them, have to stay in my past. I can love them now, I can forgive them now. But they can't hurt me anymore because they have no control over me.

This was a year in my life. It was an awesome year. It was a fantastic year. And I know without a shadow of a doubt that it's only going to get better and better. Thanks God, for loving me enough to not let me stay the way I was, and for making me a better person. Continue to help me to help others find the freedom in Christ that You have helped me to find, in the name of Jesus.

# Stop People Pleasing
**June 10**

I grew up as a people-pleaser. If someone was upset or mad, I felt it was my duty to "fix" them. I had to make things right. I don't really know when I realized this was my lot in life, but long after I was married and had my own children I discovered a very shocking revelation in my baby book. There is a section for writing various illnesses and mishaps throughout your baby's life. In one section I found, in my mother's handwriting, "Hives, caused by nerves, prescribed treatment; shot and medicine." I was six years old.

For as long as I can remember, I truly thought that living in a state of everyone yelling, and me trying to make them laugh, or just make myself invisible, was "normal." I was constantly performing. On the rare occasions when I stayed all night with friends, their homes were quiet. So quiet in fact, that I thought my friends must be in trouble. This confused me because the only time our house was quiet was when we all got sent to our rooms.

"Better a dry crust eaten in peace than a house filled with feasting and conflict." ~Proverbs 17:1 (NLT)

It wasn't until years and years later, after my own children were grown and out of the house I realized I wasted so many years trying to please the very people who could never be satisfied. Truthfully, it was not my place to satisfy them. The only thing to satisfy a restless soul is Jesus. Although I knew Him, I didn't know Him intimately until He healed me.

"...My soul magnifies and extols the Lord, And my spirit rejoices in God my Savior... For He Who is almighty has done great things for me—and holy is His name..."
~Luke 1:46-47, 49 (Amplified Bible)

Pleasing people no longer dominates my self-imposed itinerary. My agenda has become filled with pleasing the Lord. My itinerary has become filled with writing dates, because my goal is to get my story out to those who are suffering in the people-pleasing rat race.

Pleasing the Lord is not difficult. It's very simple. Get up, talk to Him, read His Word (the Bible), then do your daily tasks. When in doubt, seek His advice. Seriously. Ask God what you should do about something you are concerned about, or a decision you need to make. Seek the Lord when you're concerned about someone. If someone is giving you a hard time, tell the Lord about it. He already knows anyway, might as well talk to Him about it. He is your "Audience of One." He is the only Person you need to please.

"Finally, dear brothers and sisters, we urge you in the name of the Lord Jesus to live in a way that pleases God..."
~1 Thessalonians 4:1(a) (NLT)

My Audience of One. He is always listening to me, listening for me, watching out for me, and always ready to bless me. You may be wondering whether or not He feels the same way about you. He does. But He will not force Himself on anyone. He quietly and patiently waits for you to come to Him. Until then, He will not do anything, even though He desires to.

I may have grown up in the people pleasing rat race, but God helped me to turn off that road and onto His. He helped me because I asked Him to. He even helped me to forgive those who have hurt me. And I try to ask Him to continue helping me every day. Of course, I have days when I don't get to have my quiet time with Him and I miss it. But whenever I get a chance, I slip off and He and I have a conversation. I always feel a lot better after talking with Him.

Are you trying to please people today? Stop wearing yourself out trying to. You don't have to perform. Because God, your Audience of One, already knows what you're all about and He's crazy about you.

Shelley Wilburn

# Because I Love You
**June 30**

I wasted too many years. Plain and simple, I just wasted them. Having grown up in a very controlling, intimidating home, I grew up being a scaredy cat. I couldn't do anything right, everything was my fault, yet I never knew exactly what I did that made my family so mad. I lived in constant fear of making someone mad at me. When I married my husband, I just slid him into the role my family played in my mental and emotional state. I automatically thought that he would be the same way. He was not, is not, and never has been, yet I did not realize that.

I didn't realize it until God healed me twenty-nine years later. Why did it take so long? Why didn't God just "zap" me into healing right then and there? I wasn't ready. I had to get to a place where I knew what was causing my continual fear, anxiety, panic, and depression. I had to get to a place where I knew I had been mentally and emotionally manipulated and intimidated into being controlled. The sad thing is I was blindsided. I actually thought this was normal, yet somehow wondering how it could be so. Talk about confusion.

You see, even though I had trusted Jesus to save me thirty years beforehand, I had no idea that God had big plans for me. I didn't know that He had prepared me for, and instilled in me some great things. I still feared the people who raised me, the people whom I was supposed to be able to trust with my very life. I feared they would not approve of my life change. I even feared other people wouldn't approve. I lived in a constant state of fear and intimidation.

"For we are God's masterpiece. He has created us anew in Christ Jesus, so we can do the good things he planned for us long ago." ~Ephesians 2:10 (NLT)

But I had my priorities backwards. I loved my husband, still do, but I was still afraid to step out into our married life together for fear of what my family would say or do. Oh, my family allowed me to marry. But I couldn't leave. I was still expected to obey any and all family members and do what they said to do, not make my own decisions. I was living in a real-life "Hotel California" situation; "You can check out any time you like, but you can never leave." I was living in continual intimidation, and that is not real living.

God didn't want me to stay that way though. Instead, He gave me a loving, understanding, supportive husband. God instilled in D.A. all the patience and love that I needed to help me to grow and learn to get me to the place where my light bulb came on and I realized, "Hey! I want to be healed!" The night that happened there was a shift in my existence. God became more real, He became more of my life, and He turned me completely around.

I realized how much time I wasted with worry and fear. I went, tearfully, humbly, and repentant to my husband and said, "I'm so sorry. How could you put up with me for so long? Why didn't you ever say anything?" His reply? "Because I love you."

*Because I love you.*

He loved me so much that he willingly sacrificed to help build me up to a point where I was able to function again both mentally and emotionally, which caused me to be able to function spiritually. This is also how God is. God loves us so much that He willingly sacrificed His only Son so that we could have life, and have such a life more abundantly than we could imagine if we will only trust Him.

"The thief does not come except to steal, and to kill, and to destroy. I have come that they may have life, and that they may have it more abundantly." ~John 10:10 (NKJV)

My husband loved me enough to help me. God loves me enough to help me. God loves you enough to help you, too. He loves you, plain and simple. He loves you right where you are. In the middle of your troubles, in the middle of your mess, God loves you. He also loves you too much to leave you that way. That's why He has made a way out for you. And once you are out, you are free. The enemy will try to tell you that you have slipped back in, but don't believe him because he is a liar. Once you are free, you are "free indeed." So stay that way.

"Therefore if the Son makes you free, you shall be free indeed." ~John 8:36 (NKJV)

Don't waste another minute of your time wallowing in the mess you're in. Go to God and let Him get you out. Let Jesus free you of whatever state you're in. He doesn't want you to stay that way at all. He wants to help you, to heal you, to make you better than you've ever been before. You can ask Him why, but I'll bet He'll look at you and say: "Because I love you."

Shelley Wilburn

# Don't Back Up
**July 18**

So many times in our lives, when we are making progress, something or someone will come along and try to knock us back. In the past that happened to me a lot. Whether it was at school or at home, or somewhere in between, there were many times that I just felt like I couldn't catch a break. And I would back up. It's very frustrating.

Even though I endured much intimidation and put-downs through those times, I never stopped trying to figure out a way to get to where I knew I needed to be. That includes even the very night I went to the Lord for healing. I have learned that sometimes you just have to press through the jungle to get to the river.

I talk about healing a lot, I know. But it's crucial in what I do now, and even more important that I tell others. Because when it comes right down to it, without the healing, I wouldn't be doing what I'm doing now. I can't back up.

"I don't mean to say that I have already achieved these things or that I have already reached perfection. But I press on to possess that perfection for which Christ Jesus first possessed me." ~Philippians 3:12 (NLT)

The old saying, "You've come a long way, baby," is true even for me. While I'm not a walking billboard for cigarettes, I am a walking billboard for the Lord. I have come a long way, baby. And you can come a long way, too. Just don't back up.

I have come too far to allow someone or something to stop me in my tracks. My pastor tells us repeatedly that if you are in the will of God, nothing can touch you, not even Satan. Oh, he may think he can and he may try his hardest to mess you up, but in all reality, he has absolutely no power at all unless you give it to him.

So many times I hear Christian people complaining about their problems and "how hard it is" to do things. It really breaks my heart to hear them when I know that if they would take their eyes off the past and what is bothering them and put them back on Christ, things would begin to work out. However, I watch as they continue on a downward spiral into the black hole of un-forgiveness, bitterness, and anguish, blaming everything and everyone who crosses their path.

"No, dear brothers and sisters, I have not achieved it, but I focus on this one thing: Forgetting the past and looking forward to what lies ahead..." ~Philippians 3:13a (NLT)

I hear things like, "Well, you just don't know what *I'm* going through," It isn't directly about what you're going through. It's about where your focus lies. If you aren't focused one hundred percent on Jesus, then don't expect positive things to happen. It's that simple.

"...Let us run with endurance the race that is set before us, looking unto Jesus, the author and finisher of our faith..." ~Hebrews 12:1b-2a (NKJV)

If you aren't focused, if you have backed up, then how can you expect God to help you? However, if you are moving forward, trusting Him with everything you've got, then when the attacks come you will know what they are and how to handle them. You will walk through the fire unscathed instead of crumbling and complaining because you are under attack.

"When you go through deep waters, I will be with you. When you go through rivers of difficulty, you will not drown. When you walk through the fire of oppression, you will not be burned up; the flames will not consume you. For I am the LORD, your God, the Holy One of Israel, your Savior..." ~Isaiah 43:2-3a (NLT)

I've been there, too. I know. At some point you are going to have to ask yourself, "Is it worth it to continue to back up and let the enemy win? Or am I going to trust the One Who can get me out of it and make things better?"

Step forward today into the blessed life that God wants you to have. Start speaking positive things no matter what is going on. Speak to those things which are not as though they are. Put your foot on the neck of your enemy and declare your victory. And whatever you do, Don't Back Up!

# Grab A Hold
**September 2**

"He lifted me out of the pit of despair, out of the mud and the mire. He set my feet on solid ground and steadied me as I walked along. He has given me a new song to sing, a hymn of praise to our God..." ~Psalm 40:2-3 (NLT)

I recently had a revelation. I was looking at my calendar and noticed the passage from Psalm forty. That's when it occurred to me that this is me. This is exactly what God did for me when He healed me. I wondered how many other people are stuck in the pit of despair? How many others are stuck in the mud and mire? How many can I reach my hand out to and say, "Grab a hold! I've been sent to help you out!"

I also wonder how many would grab on and accept that hand out of the pit? Or would they look at me and say, "I've always been this way. I'll never be able to get out." Excuse me? I'm *here*! I'm holding out my hand, braced to help pull you out. Why do you want to stay down there? Oh Loves, there are many, many people with just this mentality.

These are the ones who have been intimidated for so long that they truly believe that this is their lot in life. There are people who continue telling them that they have no business out of the pit because everyone else in their family has been in the pit, it's their destiny to be there, too. Hogwash!

I was in the pit for over forty years. Kind of sounds like

the Israelites wandering in the wilderness, doesn't it? They wandered for forty years, too. But theirs was out of rebellion. Was mine? I don't know. But it doesn't matter now. What matters is that I'm out, and I'm searching for others who are in the pit so I can reach down and help them out, too.

You might be asking why I would do that. Because I believe when the Lord rescued me out of the pit, He told me this:

"The Spirit of the LORD is upon (you, Shelley), for he has anointed [you] to bring Good News to the poor. He has sent (you) to proclaim that captives will be released, that the blind will see, that the oppressed will be set free, and that the time of the LORD's favor has come." ~Luke 4:18-19, NLT (words in parentheses and brackets mine)

God's Word is full of promises for us. He has great big plans for all of us, not just a choice few. If we believe in Him, we have to believe in His Word. It never changes. It never goes out of date. Because, there is nothing new under the sun (Ecclesiastes 1:9).

My job is to help people out of the pit. I'm an encourager. I'm excited. I may come across as being a little "out there" but that's okay. I once had purple hair and I do wear mismatched socks. But the people I am getting to talk to are receptive to how I look and what I say. Why? It was ordained and anointed by God.

How many people will I get to help out? I don't know the answer to that question. But someday I will. Until then, I have to keep reaching my hand out. I have to keep searching for those who are stuck in the mud and mire. And when I meet them, I'll say, "Grab a hold!"

*Walking Healed*

# Rose-Colored Glasses
**September 4**

I'm not so color blind that I don't see or know what goes on in the world. Living with people constantly trying to intimidate me and keep me under their control, don't you know that I can spot 'em a mile away. I know the tone of voice. I know the look. I can read the body language and attitudes. I have been schooled in the "Classroom of Intimidation." But even though I have been healed of all of that and no longer allow it to control my life, don't for one minute think that I walk through life wearing rose-colored glasses.

Being healed does not mean that things are always bright and cheery. It doesn't mean that the birds always sing and the grass is always greener. The attacks still come. People still try to intimidate me. They still talk to me in a patronizing tone.

There are people who still act all blown up about something, blowing out dramatic sighs in my presence, while looking at me through their eyelashes to see if I have noticed. The difference is that I don't allow it. Frankly, most of the time I call them out on it, lovingly of course, but boldly. That surprises many, many controlling people, let me tell you. Especially when I stand there and look them square in the eye.

"Stand your ground, putting on the belt of truth and the body armor of God's righteousness." ~Ephesians 6:14 (NLT)

These situations I find so ridiculous that it literally makes me giggle. The last time someone tried to intimidate and bully me, they used the same tactics on me that they had used since I was a little girl: Yelling in a forceful voice. Since it was a phone call, I couldn't see the persons' face. But I could hear the tone; intimidation. It was meant to make me cower. It was directed at me in a way that used to cause me to give in. This time I didn't. This time I stood my ground and an amazing thing happened; the other person backed down.

"So humble yourselves before God. Resist the devil, and he will flee from you. Come close to God, and God will come close to you..." ~James 4:7-8a, (NLT)

Oh Loves, let me tell you something; the enemy uses many, many people to intimidate and control others. He will make your life miserable if it means keeping you from the wonderful promises of God. But the minute you turn around and take a stand, he gets confused. Here is where it gets even better. The victory was won over two thousand years ago, on a big, ugly, cross, when Jesus took everything in our place. Can I get a woot-woot!

There are people today who believe I walk through life wearing rose-colored glasses. I don't. My rose-colored glasses got broken the day Jesus healed me. That rosy color now comes straight from Jesus and it's the most beautiful color. Because that rosy color is from His blood, which washed me so clean that it's actually white.

I have so much color in my life now because of my healing. There is clarity. There is peace of mind. There is a fullness that I cannot explain. There is peace. There is joy, happiness, fun, boldness, and most importantly love. Trust me Lovelies, there is so much love that I can't keep quiet about all that the Lord has done and keeps doing for me. That's why I write. That's why I share.

"So if the Son sets you free, you are truly free."
~John 8:36 (NLT)

Those who wear rose-colored glasses are the ones who are blind to the truth. They walk through life every day accepting things as they are. But those who know the Truth have been set free. We don't accept things the way they are because we know that things can only get better. Why? Because, Jesus is right in the middle of it. Take off your rose-colored glasses Loves and be free.

# Zombies...the Walking Wounded
## October 21

My son Logan talks frequently about the "Zombie Apocalypse" that he and his friends (and many other people I have learned), are preparing for. And while I find it a bit comical to listen to, it hit me in church one night that quite possibly, we are already in the Zombie Apocalypse. I know this because I used to be one; a zombie.

According to Logan, a zombie is "the living dead." They kind of shuffle their way around, moan, growl, and snarl, looking for someone to attack. When they find someone they instantly grab them and bite them. If bitten by a zombie, you turn into one yourself, and the cycle repeats itself. Yet, I was healed of "Zombie-ism" when God healed me from the inside out, then gave me hope and a purpose and sent me out to help others. So there is a cure for zombies.

"The eyes of the LORD watch over those who do right; his ears are open to their cries for help... The LORD hears his people when they call to him for help. He rescues them from all their troubles." ~Psalm 34:15, 17 (NLT)

Being hurt by other people is not fun. It causes scars. I lived in a state of hurt for over forty years. At times I thought there was no hope for me. But there was. Healing was right there for the taking, if I would only receive it. Yes, I have scars. But these scars serve as a testimony to others that they too, can be healed from their wounds. They do not have to walk through life wounded, snarling, biting, grabbing, and moaning about all their troubles. In essence, a zombie the "Walking Wounded."

Here are my scars: I was put down, made fun of, ridiculed, told I was no good, shamed, made to feel guilty for everything, intimidated, controlled, and manipulated while growing up. I suffered nerve problems starting at age six, had panic and anxiety attacks, and fell into my first severe state of depression at age fifteen. I have had thoughts of suicide (but I'm a chicken thankfully and could never go through with it). I have struggled with my weight because of my emotions. Having been a pastor's wife, I have felt the sting of hateful, spiteful words, backbiting, and lies from those in the church. Each one left a mark and each one left a scar. Through it all, I was told that it was my fault. According to my family history, I probably should be in a mental institution right now. But…

God said no. God led my husband and me to a wonderful church, with wonderful people, and began to heal me. And one night, after I decided that I wanted my mind healed, God said, "It is time." Here are my scars. If you could look at them now, instead of the blinking, neon sign that said, "Easy Target" what you would see is a new sign that reads, "I survived!"

"I shall not die but live, and shall declare the works and recount the illustrious acts of the Lord...He heals my broken heart and binds up my wounds [curing my pains and sorrows]." ~Psalm 118:17 and Psalm 147:3 (Amplified Bible)

Maybe you are a zombie, too. Maybe you are among the walking wounded. You have been hurt by someone you love, someone you know, someone you go/went to church with. Maybe you are walking through life wounded, trying to find where you fit in, trying to survive long enough to get to the next place. Maybe you are hoping to find healing, just trying to stay above water and exist, yet lashing out at those who confront you.

Let me encourage you right now; don't let what others have done to you ruin your life. Because when you allow those things to continue, you let bitterness take root and grow and fester. Don't dwell on past history. Don't let all the nasty things done to you over the years make a bitter, miserable, person out of you.

"For the Scriptures say, "If you want to enjoy life and see many happy days, keep your tongue from speaking evil and your lips from telling lies. Turn away from evil and do good. Search for peace, and work to maintain it."
~1 Peter 3:10-11 (NLT)

The enemy of our souls wants us to stay miserable. He wants to keep us as zombies so that we don't prosper, so we don't help others, so we don't heal. But God wants us to move forward. Jesus wants to heal us, to pluck the bitterness out by the roots and balm over those wounds so that we can use them to help others heal, too.

Precious, don't be a zombie anymore. Don't be among the walking wounded. Come out and let Jesus heal you. Forgive. Be a survivor. Then go out and help someone else heal.

# What Are You Doing Here?
**October 23**

Sometimes, ya just want to hide.

For way too many years I ran from my issues. I ran because, to be quite frank about it, I was scared to death of the confrontation it would cause to stand up for myself. Oh, not just with people, but with myself and especially with God. Yes, I was totally afraid of God. Can you imagine that? Me, afraid of God, my loving, understanding, nurturing heavenly Daddy. But I was. All because of the intimidation of others.

Being intimidated by other people doesn't mean that I was afraid to come out in the open. I was not agoraphobic, although it would have been very easy for me to be. Staying in the safety of my home and never leaving those four walls was becoming increasingly enticing as the years went by. I wanted less and less to be around people because well, everyone I got near just seemed to feel as if they had to bash me for something or other. It's as if I had a neon sign on my forehead blinking, "Easy target!" These were all enemy attacks that I couldn't identify due to the intimidation I had lived with for so long.

You know, another person had some issues with intimidation and fear. The prophet Elijah went through some dark moments to the point that he ran and hid in a cave!*

"Elijah was afraid and fled for his life... There he came to a cave, where he spent the night. But the LORD said to him, "What are you doing here, Elijah?"
~1 Kings 19:3(a), 9 (NLT)

The odd thing about Elijah's moment of fear and doubt is that it came on the heels of a great victory. Elijah had just killed all the prophets of a false god and someone told on him. Then someone else wanted to kill him for it. Elijah heard about it, got scared, and ran.

But even though Elijah ran, God still took care of him. And when he got to the cave he decided to hide in, God was already there. Can you imagine finding the most remote place in the world to hide, thinking that your enemy can't find you there and all of a sudden you hear the voice of God say, "What are you doing here?"

You know, He does the same with us today. We run, we try to hide, and just when we think we have it made, God says, "What are you doing here?" Is there anywhere we can go that God isn't? Is there anywhere we can hide that He won't find us? No.

"O LORD, you have examined my heart and know everything about me...I can never escape from your Spirit! I can never get away from your presence!" ~Psalm 139:1, 7 (NLT)

God is everywhere, all the time. There is nowhere that you can go where He can't or won't find you, or where He isn't already. If you read all of Psalm 139, you will see that He knows everything about you, inside and out.

We may be intimidated by people around us. They may

*Walking Healed*

threaten, ridicule, and do everything they can to insult, embarrass, and make sure they ruin us publicly. But we don't have to be like Elijah and run. Instead, we can take a stand. We can smile knowing that our God is an awesome God. He will take care of us and He will also take care of our enemies.

We can be absolutely confident that no matter what anyone does, trying to attack us, they will not succeed. And anything anyone says against us will come back on them and they will be the ones who fall (see Isaiah 54:17). Why? Because His Word says so. God is on our side. He will protect and provide for us.

He did for Elijah. Then He sent him back the way he came, and gave him explicit instructions on what to do. What God told Elijah was basically that He, God, would take care of Elijah's enemies. And He will do the same for you and me today.

You and I have too much to do to allow other people to keep us hiding in the cave. So, what are you doing here? Get out of there and go back the way you came. Stand tall. Stand confident. And let God fight your battle for you.

---

\* For an in depth story of Elijah in the cave, see 1 Kings 19.

Shelley Wilburn

# Reckless
**November 22**

Sometimes I say things and my son Logan says, "Thank you, Captain Obvious!" (He loves giving his momma a hard time.) But as I sit here thinking about what my son says to me about being obvious, I am reminded that the obvious is often overlooked when serving God. Many times, He puts things out there for us and we are so caught up in our everyday lives that we miss the obvious. We need to be reckless. I want to be reckless!

What does it mean to be reckless where God is concerned? To me, it means jumping in with both feet and running with whatever it is that He has given to you. For me, that would be the healing that He did in my life. God gave me an outlet, using my love of writing, my goofiness, my silliness at times, and the newfound boldness and courage to step out with purple hair and mismatched socks and go for it.

Being reckless means stepping out in faith and recklessly following God in whatever He has commissioned you to do. There is no reason to be afraid. No reason to get anxious, apprehensive, or worried. Because if God called you to do something, you can be confident that He is going to be right with you to see it through. If He is for you, then no one or nothing can stand in your way.

*Walking Healed*

"What shall we say about such wonderful things as these? If God is for us, who can ever be against us?"
~Romans 8:31 (NLT)

For many, many years, too many years, I was afraid to step out because I was so intimidated and controlled by my emotions and the opinions of others that to be reckless in my faith was just too much for me. The tongue lashing I would get from those around me kept me frozen in place, wishing with all that was within me that I could just do something reckless. I wanted so badly to step out like I saw others doing. People like Joyce Meyer, Patsy Clairmont, Beth Moore, Anne Graham-Lotz, Priscilla Shirer and women who were stepping out and speaking up inspired me. Yet, I could only wish.

And then a beautiful thing happened. God healed me and all of a sudden, I became reckless. I started writing inspirational messages, including bits and pieces of my healing within each one. I had always loved writing for many years before my healing, but could never channel it, or find an outlet. Now here I was writing full-time.

Just a short time before God healed me, I began building a website. I decided I was going to write, but wasn't sure what. I didn't even know why. The night I was healed, I heard, "Now, write." And the words were there. Within two days www.shelleywilburn.org went live. Not only that, but while driving down the road one day, after writing that I loved wearing mismatched socks, I heard in my spirit, "Use those socks to encourage and tell others that I still love them and I can use them. I have a purpose for them, like they have for the socks."

So, the mismatched sock ministry started and people went crazy for them. But it's not about the socks. It's a reckless and outgoing way of telling people, "Hey, we are all different. And just like these socks still have a purpose, God has a purpose for you."

"For I know the plans I have for you," says the LORD. "They are plans for good and not for disaster, to give you a future and a hope." ~Jeremiah 29:11 (NLT)

But how could I segue into telling someone that without just blurting it out? I needed something to get people to talk to me without scaring them off before I could tell them how much Jesus loves them, wants to heal them, and has a purpose for them. Do you know He gave me that, too?

My daughter Katie, came in one day with hot pink highlights in her bangs. They were beautiful. But a week later, she colored them back to her natural hair color because she felt that she just couldn't pull it off. It really bothered her. And that's when I heard, "So you get purple in your hair."

What?! Purple? Really? That is really reckless. Hey wait a minute; if I have purple hair, that would be really obvious, and people will see that and maybe say something. And I heard, "There is your segue." So, I did it and it worked. Talk about reckless. What grandmother do you know who wears mismatched socks and colors her hair purple?

That would be me. Reckless. Since God healed me, He gave me a writing outlet. He gave me a voice. He gave me mismatched socks. And yes, He even gave me purple hair for a time (although I had to have someone put it in there for me). But it's all part of the reckless way that I follow Him.

How are you being reckless for God? What obvious thing has He given you that makes you stand out and be a sold-out, reckless, child of the King? I'd love to hear your reckless story.

Here's how you can connect with me:

E-mail me at shelley@shelleywilburn.org.
Follow me on Facebook at
www.facebook.com/authorshelleywilburn
Twitter @Shelley_Wilburn
Pinterest at www.pinterest.com/shelleyawilburn
Follow me at my website at www.shelleywilburn.org

Shelley Wilburn

# Unlocking Your Door
**December 23**

A very dear friend of mine gave me a gift a while back: a lovely little journal. I love journals. This one is red and it is tied closed with a piece of red suede. But I think the most precious thing about this gift is that tied to the journal is an antique skeleton key.

The key is pitted, dingy, bent, and twisted. It has been used and a little abused. But this little key means more to me than just a key. And it means more to me than just what my friend gave it to me for.

We had recently finished a wonderful Bible study by Priscilla Shirer entitled, *Gideon* (I would highly recommend this study if you are looking to discover how God can use your weaknesses to do mighty things). One of the lessons in the study talked about how our weakness is the key to God's strength. It is the key to unlock the door to whatever it is that God is calling you to do. However, once unlocked you must open the door.

I began to think about that and when I saw the skeleton key, I immediately sent my friend a text and told her how much I loved her gift, especially the key. Her reply; "I chose that key specifically for you. That key was the only one in the batch I got that was bent. As soon as I saw it, I knew it was to go to you. And I mean that in every good way!"

It may seem trivial to some people, but to me that key

represented a lot of things in my life. I'm a little bent and twisted myself from all the things I've been through in my life. I mentioned to my friend, just that and the fact that the key still has a purpose just like we all do. She agreed.

We all go through various trials, hardship, and things in our lives. Some are extremely hurtful and they scar us and bend and twist us. We get pitted, just like my little key. But the amazing thing about that is the fact that long before we ever went through any of that, God knew it was going to happen. He knew the things we would go through. He also knew that those things we call our weaknesses would be the very things that He would use within us to show His strength. What does that mean? It means that He is going to use those things through us to help others find the hope that we have found.

Yes, I've been hurt deeply by other people. I have been wounded and scarred both mentally and emotionally. But God healed me of that and when He did, He turned me around and said, "Now, use that to help other women find hope that they are not alone. Help them find Me. Show them that they have a purpose. Show them My love. Show them the way out." These were not audible words, but a strong desire in my heart. I knew that this is what I was supposed to do. God used my key and unlocked the door. But I had to open it and step through.

"Shift your focus from the key itself to the door God can unlock with it. Use what you have, no matter how weak—and God will take care of the rest." ~From *Gideon*, by Priscilla Shirer, Lifeway Christian Resources, 2013

There are so many things going on in the world today, such as financial problems, sickness, wars over religions, and many other things that vie for our attention and our emotions. But you don't have to be the victim of them. People are going to say and do hurtful things. They are going to say things about you that are not true. They are going to try to convince others that what they are saying is the truth. It's up to you to show them the real Truth. Jesus.

Most of my scars are from the past. However, just because God healed me doesn't mean that I don't still run up against people who want to cause hurt, because I do. I am. And that's okay. My key is still helping me to unlock new doors. And I am still helping others learn to use their keys.

Don't focus on your weaknesses as something that hinders you. Instead, let God use them to unlock the doors to what He has in store for you. You may just find something beautiful behind your next door.

# God's Favor...is NOW!
**December 29**

I was asked to speak to a group of people a while back. When I received the invitation, I had no idea what I was going to say to them. But as time progressed, I felt the Holy Spirit impress upon me to speak to them about God's favor. Truthfully, it came to me one night around eleven o'clock, right as I was trying to fall asleep (the Holy Spirit is like that, but He knows I'm a night owl so it's all good).

**God's Favor**

The reason for speaking on this is that God wants us to know that His favor is now. God is raising up an army of women now. Here's why; women are being used, abused, and thrown aside like trash. They are treated as such, made to think as such, and are the victims of many abuses such as verbal, mental, emotional, physical, sexual...women and girls are being sold into human trafficking. They are victims of pornography, prostitution, drugs and alcohol. God's favor is upon several woman who have been rescued, healed, or brought out of some form of many of the above mentioned things, and He has sent them out to give others hope. I know. I am one of them.

"The Spirit of the Lord is upon me, for he has anointed me to bring Good News to the poor. He has sent me to proclaim that captives will be released, that the blind will see, that the oppressed will be set free, and that the time of the Lord's favor has come." ~Luke 4:18-19 (NLT)

The day I realized what was causing my issues with depression, I realized that I needed my mind to be healed from the hurt and the abuse that I had endured for way too long. It was a turning point in my life because the next week God literally healed me from the inside out. But He didn't leave me at just healed. He directed me to the new path He had waiting for me.

He has a path especially for you, too. No matter your background. No matter your circumstances. God has something in mind for you. He always has. Everything God has planned for you is good. The problem is that there is also an enemy out there who doesn't want you to find your God-given plan. And he will do everything he can think of to keep you from finding that healing and that purpose. But one thing he doesn't know is that he has no power unless you give it to him. So, if you are believing the lies, the negative, hurtful things that people say and do to you, then the enemy is keeping you from God's favor.

"For we are God's masterpiece. He has created us anew in Christ Jesus, so we can do the good things he planned for us long ago." ~Ephesians 2:10 (NLT)

My friend Karla Akins*, was doing a Saturday blog post about Strong Girls. She is also one of God's Warrior Princesses who is diligently working to help others find the purpose God has for them. She is sincerely trying to help girls and women find freedom in healing and helping them discover who God says they are. I encourage you to check out her blog as well and find encouragement.

God has something special for you my dear sisters. Trust me on this, and trust God. You have something special to offer to other girls and women, to give them encouragement and hope that there is something better out there. Don't be a victim any longer. God's favor is now. He is waiting for you with open arms.

*Karla Akins is the best-selling author of several historical biographies, novels and more. When she's not writing, you may find her zooming down the road on her motorcycle or looking for treasure. You can find Karla's posts about Strong Girls by visiting her website at www.karlaakins.com/category/strong-girls.

# Far Out!
**January 27, 2014**

Sometimes, God gives us some far out orders. Some of His promises are way out there and well, they just seem too far out to comprehend or believe. Don't they?

God told Abraham that his wife, Sarah, would have a baby. When Sarah heard it, she laughed. I mean, she was in her nineties, so I guess that promise really seemed far out. But then she conceived and had Isaac. (Genesis 18:1-15)

When the Angel of the Lord appeared to Gideon and told him that he would fight against his enemies and win, Gideon asked for a sign to be sure he heard it right. After he got the sign, he asked for another sign just to make extra sure (Judges 6:33-40). And when he went to battle against thousands of Midianites with only three hundred men he won.

The Angel of the Lord (Gabriel) appeared to Zechariah and told him that his wife, Elizabeth would conceive and have a son. Instead of belief, Zechariah questioned and was struck silent until Elizabeth delivered their son, John the Baptist (Luke 1:5-23) Pretty far out!

At the same time Elizabeth was carrying her baby, Mary was visited by Gabriel and given the message from God that she would conceive and carry God's Son, Jesus. What's so far out about that promise is that Mary was a virgin. But instead of questioning the validity of the promise, Mary just wanted to know how it was going to happen since she was indeed a virgin. The angel was all too happy to explain it (Luke 1:26-38).

When God healed me, He gave me a promise, too. He told me through a very godly man, that I would minister to women and give them encouragement and hope. My initial thought was, "Oh God, not *them*!" But God's answer was, "Yes. Them." Women were my intimidators. Many of them were the ones who hurt me the most, who kept me in misery, who judged me the worst. Yet they are the exact ones God sent me back into the ring to fight for (Luke 4:18-19). What a far out promise. What a far out task.

Each one of the above people received a far out promise from God, including me. And each far out promise was backed up and fulfilled. God is in the promise making/promise fulfilling business. He never breaks a promise. He never goes back on His word. And you can bet that if He told you to do something or that you will do something, it will happen.

When God healed me, I never dreamed that what I would be doing would be ministering to the very people who intimidated me the most. Yet, I am. Not only that, but I also get to meet many more women who are broken and hurting just like I was and I am able to tell them that there is hope for them, just like there was hope for me.

What good would my healing be if I never shared it? What good would yours be if you never shared it? Hurting people hurt other people, it's true. But healed people help hurting people find hope and healing through the capable hands of Jesus. This is my calling. This is what I do. I'm not a counselor, I'm just one of the called. And that is far out!

Shelley Wilburn

# Rescuing People
**February 18**

I watch hopelessly quite often as various people flit from one friend to another, to another, looking for someone to satisfy their needs, only to come up unsatisfied and move onto the next. While that person moves on, the one who was just left is standing there wondering, "What just happened?" The sad conclusion to this saga is that the unsatisfied person will remain unsatisfied. They will also continue to lay blame with every other person they proclaim to have had to sever ties with because they will ultimately and sincerely believe in their minds that the other person was to blame. It's always someone else's fault, never their own.

While this is a sad tale, it is very true. I lived it for many years. I flit from one friend to another, to another, always looking for approval, justification, pity, acceptance, whatever I could get to make me feel better, to make me feel that someone, anyone understood where I was coming from. Instead, what I got was at first friendship, then impatience. It always seemed as if my friends turned against me and sought new friends. In my mind, something must have been wrong with them because I was sure I didn't do anything wrong. They just didn't understand me. But it was a little of both and mostly me. What I needed was to go to the Lord with my issues instead of going to everyone else and bombarding them with all my troubles.

I'm not saying talking to a friend isn't wise. If you have a friend who is a good listener and encourages you, then by all means, confide in them. But don't expect them to fix you, because they can't. Only God can do that. And that brings me to my lowest of lows and my rock bottom epiphany that ultimately led me to where I am today.

I was so beat down by my past and intimidated by the people in my surroundings that I could not get past the hurt long enough to find a real friend. Nor could I allow myself to trust them. I just lumped them all into the same category and expected them to eventually turn on me and hurt me. Not all of them were like that. Hurting people hurt people. But rescued people rescue people.

When God healed me, He literally fixed me from the inside out. I didn't have to rely on someone else to pour out my troubles to, to give me justification, pity, acceptance, or anything else to make me feel better. Because when God healed me, He gave me justification. He gave me acceptance. He gave me everything I needed, fixed my brokenness, sanctified me, and then turned me around and gently nudged me in this direction and said, "Now, go give your sisters hope. Tell them what I've done for you. Tell them I can heal them too, and then send them My way." So here I am.

I am on a new path. Since being on this path, I have encountered many sisters along the way. Some of them have been receptive. Some of them, not so much. What breaks my heart is when one of them sees me as anything but a positive influence. My heart hurts so bad to watch them flit from one friend to another, to another, seeking approval, acceptance, justification, and that "please feel sorry for me" attitude that I myself once portrayed. Because I know that within a few short weeks, she will throw that friendship away and move on to another new friend, seeking the same things once again, leaving hurt and destruction in her wake.

This is how the enemy blindsides us into believing that people can fix our problems. We hesitate to go to the Lord for our heart surgery, instead talking things out with friends because our friends get us, they approve of us, and they accept us how we are. In essence, they enable us to continue on our path of destruction. All the while, God is waiting to take us in. He doesn't leave us in the same place we are. He makes us move out of our comfort zone and into the life that He has planned for us.

Sometimes though, we get so comfortable in our misery that we would just rather stay there and wallow because we're getting more attention there than if we were to move out to where the Lord wants to use us. We want what we want, justifying ourselves by saying, "I'm waiting for God to answer me." Well honey, God *is* answering you. He's saying, "Hey, come over here. I have something wonderful for you." Yet we won't move.

Be encouraged today. Had I not moved from where I was and stepped out in faith, determined to get my mind healed, you would not be reading this right now. No, it's not arrogance. It isn't pride. This is healing. This is what happens when God steps in and changes your life. What you see and read here is the result of the healing hand of God in my life. I no longer go from one friend to another to another seeking approval, justification, and all those other things. I got all of that and more the night I asked God to heal me and received everything He had waiting for me.

"And whatever things you ask in prayer, believing, you will receive." ~Matthew 21:22 (NKJV)

You have a mighty big present waiting for you, too. Will you step out and go for it? Or stand back and watch from the sidelines?

Shelley Wilburn

# Discovering My More
**April 17**

I heard these words recently, "You are more than you know, and God is much more than you know." Profound words, and they're true. You are more than you know and God is so much more than we could ever know. Right after I heard those words, the next words were, "And people are more than we allow them to be."

How then, can we discover the more in us? Where is it? Where does it come from? How do we access it? The answer may elude us, it may seem as if there is no answer, or it may even seem beyond our reach. But it isn't. The answer is just a breath away. It's just a prayer away. It comes from God, and we access our more simply by asking God for it.

There are so many women today who don't believe that they are more than they know. They don't believe that they have what it takes for anything. They don't believe God could ever use them for anything spectacular. They think their past is too much for God to allow them to be part of anything, good or otherwise. Sadly, they are very, very wrong. Even sadder still, many of them never discover their more and go through life wishing that things would have been different. They live in the "if only" section of their lives always dreaming, never bringing those dreams to reality.

But God has so much more for us!

"Behold, I am the LORD, the God of all flesh. Is there anything too hard for Me?" ~Jeremiah 32:27 (NKJV)

I lived for so many years in the "if only" section of my life. I had been beaten down and ridiculed for so long by others that I just didn't think there was really anything spectacular to my life. Just be a quiet stay-at-home mom, raise your kids, take care of your grandkids, and live your life. That's fine. I don't mind that at all. But I absolutely knew that there was more, yet it was just out of my reach. I didn't know how to get to it because everyone else around me other than my husband kept me pinned down mentally, emotionally, and spiritually.

Listen, if God is calling you to do something and you know it, step out in faith in Him and go for it. Because if God is calling you out, you can know right now that He will equip you to succeed. It isn't hard for Him, and it's definitely not hard for you. No one and I mean no one can tell you that you can't do it. They can't keep you from doing it, because it's a Divine Calling. That is between you and the Most High God. No one can dispute it. No one can negate it.

My calling is to write and speak my story to give hope and healing to others. No one else can tell me I can't do it. No one else can prevent me from doing it. Oh they can try, but let me tell you something else, whatever God calls you to do no one can stand in your way either.

"No weapon formed against you shall prosper and every tongue that rises against you shall fall." ~Isaiah 54:17a

Shelley Wilburn

(NKJV, paraphrased)

You are more than you know. But the only way you're going to discover your more is by stepping out in faith and asking God to show you. Then walk in that anointing He pours out on you. I promise you will never look back once you discover your more.

# Snakes in the Garden
**July 19**

Have you ever walked out into your garden, or any garden for that matter, and come upon a snake? That's enough to give your heart palpitations! I'm not fond of snakes. In fact, I hate them. Yes, I know that some snakes are good for the garden, good for your yard, and eat mice and other not-so-lovely creatures. But they also eat the good ones too and will hide in the grass waiting to strike you when you least expect it. So I'm not fond of them. My husband dislikes them even more than I do, and he will go as far as to tell you that he hates them too.

You know, a snake (serpent) is what the devil disguised himself as in the Garden of Eden when he pulled one over on Eve, and then Adam (see Genesis 3). Isn't that just like an enemy? Disguise himself as something else in order to trick you into thinking or acting a certain way, or to get you to mess up.

For years, he tricked me into believing that I was no good. He tricked me into believing that my life didn't matter, that no one cared about me, that I was useless, and most of all, that God didn't have any use for me either. So, why even try? Why even get out of bed in the morning? No one was going to defend me. No one was going to care. No one was going to like me, love me, or help me. Wrong!

For too many years I had listened to one snake after another tell me I couldn't, I shouldn't, and I wouldn't. But

God said I could, I should, and I would. He knew before I was even born that I would be writing this right now. The enemy knew I would and tried to prevent it. But he doesn't have any power. For too many years though I allowed him to control me, until I discovered that he only had power because I gave it to him. Not anymore!

The enemy is a sneaky, vile, snake who is waiting to strike when you least expect it. You need to put your foot down right on top of Satan and take control back. You may be wondering how to do that. Let me explain; all you have to do is make up your mind, and tell him no. Then ask the Lord to fill you with peace, comfort, and a sound mind, because the truth is that you do not have a spirit of fear. You do have power, love, and a sound mind though (2 Timothy 1:7).

It's time to get the snakes out of your garden.

# Changing Your Life
**October 16**

There are many people, even friends of mine, who have been or are suffering with anxiety and depression. It breaks my heart, especially when I hear them say, "It runs in my family," or "I just deal with it and battle it every day, hoping for the best."

I can totally identify with this, which is why it hurts my heart so much for them. The biggest reason is because I suffered in silence with this very thing for over forty years.

Anxiety, depression, panic attacks, low self-esteem, no self-worth, oppression, and intimidation were among my constant companions. I didn't like any of them, yet it seemed as if everywhere I went, they followed me. Many times they came straight from the people I was closest to. Quite often they would embarrass me so badly that I had to leave whatever place I was at, while ridicule and insults from others followed me out the door. Sometimes I would be told I was not allowed to leave but had to stay and listen to what the people attacking me called truth. Many times they called me on the phone after I got home to continue the diatribe.

I thought this was just how life was meant to be. I honestly thought that the hopeless feelings I had were just life. It ran in the family, so why wouldn't I have it? My grandmother and mother had depression, I heard them talk openly about it my whole childhood. They spoke it over me continually, "Just wait till you get older. This is what you have to look forward to. It runs in the family."

"Better a dry crust eaten in peace than a house filled with feasting—and conflict." ~Proverbs 17:1(NLT)

    People with depression and anxiety suffer. But they also cause those around them to suffer too, whether they mean to or not. In my family, those who were suffering weren't content unless everyone else was upset and anxious as well. And while there was medication for this problem, no one ever told any of us that God was not the author of our misery. Yet, I know that I often questioned Him as to why He allowed me to have this malady.
    God did not give any of us depression, anxiety, or any other emotional or mental disorder. However, sometimes He does allow us to go through these things. The answer though, is not always readily available. But one thing I do know is that though we suffer through the "black hole" or the "pit" as some like to call it, God is always using this to move us forward into the calling He has for our lives.
    You can be healed from depression, panic, anxiety, oppression, and all the above mentioned things. God has a purpose for you, dear lovelies. He loves you most dearly, is crazy about you, and He does have a use and purpose for your life.

"The LORD will work out his plans for my life— for your faithful love, O LORD, endures forever. Don't abandon me, for you made me." ~Psalm 138:8 (NLT)

    You are not hopeless. You are not a mistake. Your

circumstances are not fixed or resigned to "it runs in the family." It's time to lift your head and take a stand. Receive the healing of God over your mind, your emotions, your body, and all aspects of your life. Walk out your healing. Just because something "runs in the family" doesn't mean that it continues with you. Break the cycle. Break the chains. Break the curse. Don't let your history destroy your destiny.

"I cry out to God Most High, to God who will fulfill his purpose for me. He will send help from heaven to rescue me, disgracing those who hound me. My God will send forth his unfailing love and faithfulness." ~Psalm 57:2-3 (NLT)

I'm not saying flush all your medications.* I'm also not saying that medicine is bad, because you may just need that for a while. Find a good, Christian counselor. That's not so bad either and they may help you work out your healing. Just remember that God is the Great Physician, the Healer, and the name of Jesus is above all other names...including depression.

Thank God for healing you today. Read His Word on healing. Speak it over your life today and every day. Trust me, they are very powerful. God's Word does not return void (Isaiah 55:11). Don't spend one more minute suffering anxiety. Read the healing prayer below and begin a new, healed life.

*In the name of Jesus I bind depression, anxiety, panic, oppression, and every other malady associated with these things, and I cast them into the depths of the sea, never to return. I loose the Holy Spirit into my life to fill the holes left by these things. I release peace, a sound mind, calmness, and peace of mind. I take captive every thought. I thank You Lord for healing me, and I receive that and walk in it. No weapon formed against me shall prosper, and every tongue that rises against me shall fall. I do not have a spirit of fear. I have power, love, and a sound mind. I am the head and not the tail. I am more than a conqueror through Christ Who loves me, and I can do all things through the strength that He gives me. Thank you, Lord for hearing me. I claim all Your promises, in Jesus' name, Amen and AMEN!*

If that's you today, please email me. I'll be happy to pray for you, and send you more information on healing. You can change your life, live healed, and walk in that healing.

*I am not an advocate of discontinuing medication for depression or anxiety cold turkey. Please seek medical advice, and above all pray first before doing anything. Make sure you have clear guidance from the Lord but also talk to your doctor or counselor.

# Where Do I Go From Here?

I've been asked a lot of questions about my healing. Many of those questions come from people wanting to know what was I really like before the healing, since looking at me now, most people can't believe I ever suffered depression much less have anxiety attacks. They even have a hard time believing that I was once so intimidated by other people that I couldn't function in public very well.

One thing I try to tell people is that I hid it. I was a master of disguise. I played a one-woman charade for the better part of forty years. Only two people saw right through that into the scared, hurt, person that I was; God and my husband. Granted, at age sixteen, he was my then soon-to-be boyfriend. Still, he saw me. You have to understand that. He saw me way back in high school and still saw the real me through the tough-girl façade, the harsh, smart-mouth, and cocky attitude. They were all a ruse, an act, a bluff to keep people at a distance and from hurting me. Most of the time, they all backfired on me, getting me into a lot of trouble.

People who meet me now usually have the same reaction to what I just mentioned above, "I can't believe you were ever like that." Believe me. It's true.

One day I had a young woman approach me after a Bible study where I shared a little bit of my healing story. She looked at me and said, "I just thought you've always had it all together." I smiled, then laughed a bit. Then I told her no, that in fact if she had known me just a couple of years earlier, she would have seen a totally different Shelley.

So what happens after the healing? Is everything hunky-dory? Does everything run smoothly? Is life just peachy-keen and perfect? Not by a long shot. There are still trials. There are still moments of frustration. And of course there are still people who want to try to shut me up. There are still people who want to intimidate me, threaten me, ridicule me, and try to convince others that I'm not what I say I am. I find this very sad because these people don't really know me.

The difference now is that these people don't usually get a second thought. In years past, I would have run, gotten upset, sunk lower into depression, my self-esteem would have plummeted, and or I would have ended up having a very heated confrontation with the person or persons who were doing these things. Ultimately I would have quit trying altogether, thinking that if someone was against me then maybe I really was doing the wrong thing. I had my thinking completely backwards.

I have received messages and letters from people trying to drag me into drama. But this is how I determine whether or not this is something I need to give my personal attention. Maybe this will help you as well. There are three things I consider when someone is trying to give me advice or tell me what they think I should do:

1) Is it positive? If it isn't positive, I don't mess with it. Negativity is not something I need in my life. It only drags me down. It steals my joy, causes stress, and prevents me from moving forward. So if it's not positive, I drop it like a hot potato. Even if it's said in a joking way.

2) Is it helpful? If someone wants to tell me something or give me advice, I'll be polite and listen. However if it begins with, "I think you should," or "I don't think you should," then I'm very careful. Usually, if it's not helpful, it will also be negative. However, people who are sincere will not tell you what to do, they will suggest a, "You might want to think about…" Listen with open ears.

3) Is it godly? This one is a big one with me. If it's not godly then it's gossip. If someone is a godly person, they will give godly advice. Their advice will also coincide with number two above. You can trust what they have to say. The Holy Spirit will guide you with this one especially. Godly wisdom and godly advice are very important. If you are prayed up and in tune with the Holy Spirit, you will definitely know the difference between godly and gossip and can avoid unnecessary setbacks.

You may have to separate yourself from various people. Trust me when I say that separating yourself from certain people who continually try to keep you oppressed, or intimidate you into backing down from something you have dreamed of doing, or something you know God is calling you to do is not only a big step, it's also scary. But whatever anyone tells you it is not petty. It's biblical. There will be those who want to convince you that they are Christians, but act totally opposite. These are they who feel threatened by what you are embarking on. Love them, yet keep your distance.

When God heals you, you're healed. Period. The Bible

says that who the Son sets free is free indeed. That means there's no going back to the old you. Those chains and shackles were broken to pieces so you could never put them back on. There's no reason for me to go back to the way things used to be.

In the Bible study Gideon, by Priscilla Shirer, she states that "you are not who you used to be so you have no business going where you used to go." This statement is truer than you realize. Why would you go back into the pit if God just pulled you out and gave you a new life? Yet there will be those who will try to push you back in. Your job now is to not let them.

It almost happened to me. I nearly fell back into the pit once until I realized that, wait a minute; God healed me! I am free. This person did not accept my testimony or my offer of help. Instead, they took what I had said and twisted it, then tried to corrupt what God had done in my life. For a while it bothered me. But then I woke up one day and realized that this was a spiritual attack, and I took the necessary measures; Prayer.

Not that I didn't pray before, I did. I just changed my prayer tactic. Forgiveness is a great tool. It doesn't take anyone off the hook. It just switches hooks, from mine to God's, which is what I did. Then I moved on.

You have to learn to move on and not dwell on things that try to get you down. By dwelling on it, you give it legs to walk around and arms to hit you with. In other words, you allow it to grow. You allow it to control you, to intimidate you, and to manipulate you. All these things prevent you from moving into the arena that God has prepared for you. It's a tactic of the enemy to keep you motionless.

*Walking Healed*

It took me a while to figure out what to do next, after my healing. Do I keep writing? Do I try to get speaking engagements? How do I let others know that God healed me? The answer to those came very quickly. The writing, you already know, was an open floodgate. I had no problem with that. The speaking engagements, though few and far between, started coming in. But my issue with that was what do I talk about each time? That too, was taken care of rather quickly when I realized that it's always about what God has done for me. It's always about the healing, because that's my story. It needs to be told whether I write it or speak it.

The biggest question I had was how do I let others know that God healed me? It was four days after my healing when I got that answer. I got it from the back seat of the motorcycle I ride with my husband.

We have a very unique motorcycle ministry and it was on that motorcycle that God opened my eyes and heart. I won't go into that ministry here, that's for another time but you can learn about it at www.where2.org. When God healed me, it was spoken over me that I would minister to women, that they would come to me and I would tell them my story. I wondered. Yet, God literally showed me that prophecy.

Every time we would stop while out on our motorcycle, my husband would always have people approach him to ask questions about the trailer we pull. It's a casket. It's just a prop we use to encourage people to know Jesus before they get in one of those things. But my husband was always much better at talking to people than I was because I just couldn't do it before. However, one particular day something changed.

We had got off the bike and I watched as my husband

started talking to someone who walked up and asked about the casket. While I watched, I got the feeling someone was looking at me. I turned and there stood a woman, staring at me. I wore a full-face helmet at the time, so I raised the face shield and smiled at her. That's all it took for her to open up and before long I was sharing my healing testimony with her.

I say that it was the oddest thing to have someone stare at me like they needed to tell me something, but I know now that it was God. One by one, every stop we made, there was at least one woman, sometimes more who would approach me. They would stare at me. Then I would speak, and they would begin talking. Before long, they were telling me things that were very personal. But those things gave me an opening to reveal my healing story.

When these women would hear the small testimony I gave them, it changed everything. Some would smile. Some would cry. But all of them did the same physical thing: they hugged me. Before I let them go though, I would give them a small gift, a pair of mismatched socks. These socks represent what God did in my life. They are also a reminder that none of us match. We are all different. Yet we all have a purpose, just like these socks. We don't have to match. God made us all different, but he can still use us. The socks are a reminder of that. They still have a purpose too.

So, where do I go from here? Up baby, up! Always forward. Always pressing on. Remember that. You move forward, too. Onward and upward, always working your way toward the ultimate prize, when we hear Jesus say, "Well done, good and faithful servant."

# Parting Words

We have come to the end of our walk together. My how time has flown by! I hope you have enjoyed our walk. It has been a pleasure to get to walk along with you, giving you hope that the Lord is with you on your own walk. He never leaves us and never forsakes us, and He's the best walking buddy we could ever have.

Before I go, I just want to give you a little more encouragement as you go your way and I go mine.

Every day is a new day. Every day is a new adventure. I try to look at things this way. Since the Bible says that God's mercies are new every day, I try to remember that and live in the moment He has given me. Yes, there will be people who rub me the wrong way. There will be people who don't agree with me, or believe me. I can't worry about that. I don't have time. All I can do is move forward and hope for the best, not only for me but for them. And there are some people that I just can't let myself be worried about.

We all have a story to tell. We all have a journey to walk. When we put Christ first in our lives, seek His wise counsel, and put it into practice, our lives will be richer and more abundant than we could ever imagine.

Never let anyone try to tell you that you talk too much about what the Lord has done for you. You are not being arrogant or prideful about it if you keep yourself humble enough to give God the credit for what has happened in your life. Yes, the Lord healed me. I'll never get over that, because what He healed me from made a major difference in my life. I can't be still about that.

Walk your walk, dear lovelies. Shout it from the rooftops if you can. However you can tell your story, tell it. Someone somewhere needs to hear it. If my story has helped you or encouraged you in any way, I want to hear from you. I want to pray for you. You can connect with me on Facebook, Twitter, Pinterest, and my website. Let me know how God ministered to you through the pages of my story.

Until we meet again, either here or in our Heavenly Home, know that wherever you are we are siblings in Christ.

Love you, my dear ones!

# About the Author

Shelley Wilburn and her husband D.A. live in a house they built together on five and a half acres they lovingly call their Rinky Dink Farm. Along with their moody little dog Buster, they love to raise chickens, ride motorcycles, and watch the wild deer and turkeys cross their field. Shelley and D.A. have three grown, married children and three grandsons.

Shelley began writing when she was twelve years old. She wrote on the Junior High School newspaper but didn't follow her love of writing until years later. She secretly wrote poetry but never let anyone read her poems, keeping them hidden in a notebook. She has written several articles for various newspapers, women's magazines, and newsletters but didn't start writing full time until God healed her. That's when she knew that writing was her full-time calling.

Shelley tells of the complete change God has done in her life through her ministry, on her website and through the motorcycle ministry she and her husband share. Using her love of writing, motorcycle riding, and wearing mismatched socks, Shelley has developed a unique ministry of encouraging others using biblical truths and stories from her own personal life.

Shelley loves to hear from her readers.

You can find Shelley at

Her website: www.shelleywilburn.org,
Her ministry website: www.where2.org,
Facebook: www.facebook.com/authorshelleywilburn
Twitter: @Shelley_Wilburn
Pinterest at www.pinterest.com/shelleyawilburn
E-mail her at shelley@shelleywilburn.org.

# Appendix A
**Keeping a Prayer Journal**

If you have ever kept a diary, you can keep a prayer journal. By writing your prayers in a journal, you are more focused on what you are praying for. You can also keep the dates of when you prayed, then go back later and record the date God answered your prayer. It's truly amazing to see how He blesses you by reading back through the things you prayed about and when He answered.

A prayer journal doesn't have to be a fancy book. It can be anything from a stenographer's notebook, binder with loose leaf paper you can add to, hardback, softback, spiral notebook, or a leather-bound book. Anything that holds paper will do for your journal. It's up to your taste. Be creative.

I recommend starting out simple. Write the date. You can be as formal or informal as you want with the Lord, as long as you're honest and up front with Him. He loves to hear from you. Talk to Him as you would your best friend. After all, He *is* your Best Friend.

However you choose to address Him, be consistent. When I first learned to journal my prayers, I felt awkward at first. I wasn't comfortable. But then I realized that the Bible is basically God's love letter to me. Why couldn't my prayer journal be my love letter back to Him? It can. The more I wrote, the better I got at it.

At first, my prayers were short paragraphs. I started out by saying, "Dear Lord" or "Heavenly Father" and went from there. Just a few lines at first because I really didn't know I could actually tell Him everything on my heart. After that, I wrote more and more, filling more and more pages. My prayers went from one page to four or five. My beginnings went from "Dear Lord" to "Good Morning, Lord" or "Thank You, Jesus." I was getting more and more comfortable with His presence. And yes, when I wrote to Him, He showed up.

Tell Him about your day. Tell Him about people you're concerned with. Tell Him about who has made you happy, hurt you, made you sad, or made you angry. Tell Him about your kids, your grandkids, your husband, and your friends. Tell Him how you feel. Tell Him about things that bother you. Tell Him everything. He already knows. He's just waiting for you to trust Him with all of it. Repeat His Word back to Him. Remind Him of His promises to you.

Over the years, I've learned that it doesn't matter how you talk to the Lord, as long as you talk to Him. I've been guilty of not talking to Him. And I've learned that by not talking to Him, I suffer. However, when I go to Him, say I'm sorry, and ask Him to forgive me I find He's right there waiting. He forgives me and I'm right back in close relationship with Him once again.

Keep your prayer journal wherever you sit to have your quiet time with Him. Make sure your family knows that this is your private book that only you and God look at. It's your conversations with Him. When you fill one up, get yourself another. But make sure you keep your journals. Always look back through and make more notes. You'll get a blessing from reading them.

Lastly, when God answers a prayer, be sure to thank Him. Let Him know that you remember, too.

Prayer journals are very easy to manage and to write. Once you get the hang of it, you'll be hooked. I know. I've been doing it fifteen years.

# Appendix B
## How to Handle Confrontation

It's guaranteed that at some point in your life you will have a confrontation with someone. You'll probably have more than one. The key is, don't panic. Below are some guidelines on how to handle a confrontation.

1. **Remain calm.** Someone who wants to intimidate by confrontation will try to upset you at the start. By staying calm, you have let them know that they are not going to control you or the situation.
2. **Maintain eye contact.** When you don't look others in the eye, you are letting them know that they intimidate you. This gives them the upper hand and allows them to bully you and/or control you. Eye contact also helps you to gauge the other person's actions and mood.
3. **Smile.** It might sound silly, but when you smile you look happy. If you look happy, you will be happy. For someone who is confrontational, intimidating, or controlling, this is off-putting. Generally it causes the confrontation to backfire, or makes the other person confused.
4. **Speak kindly.** Use your words well. When you speak, be kind, be gentle, and be loving. It might be difficult especially if the person who confronts you is being negative, agitated, or harsh. Saying things like, "I'm sorry you feel that way" or "That must really be tough" might help defer the confrontation if the other person

feels that you're empathetic or sympathetic. However, do not be patronizing (condescending).

5. **Stand up for yourself.** If the person causing the confrontation becomes insulting, judgmental, or accusing and is just trying to cause hurt, stand up for yourself and put a stop to it. You do have a right to tell him or her to stop. If he continues, it's time for you to walk away. There will be people like this in your life at times.

6. **Pray for that person.** You may not be able to pray for them while you're with them. But do make an effort to pray for them when you're alone. Tell the Lord about them and give the entire situation to Him. Write about it in your prayer journal, or just have a good heart-to-heart with your Heavenly Father.

Confrontations are not always negative. They can also be positive. By putting your best foot forward and making sure you stay positive, any confrontation you may have can and will come out for the better.

Shelley Wilburn

# Notes

**My Journey to Forgiveness**
1. Romans 12:2, John 10:10, NKJV

**Breaking the Chains**
2. Luke 4:18 Amplified Bible

**Mending Fences**
3. Psalm 16:11, Romans 16:17-18, Matthew 18:15, NKJV
4. Peter 5:8-9, HCSB

**Offense and Defense**
5. Matthew 6:12, NKJV (The Lord's Prayer)
6. Galatians 5:1, HCSB
7. James 4:7b, Ephesians 6:13, NKJV

**Revelation to Revolution**
8. Isaiah 14:12-16 (Fall of Lucifer)
9. Hebrews 1:5-7, NKJV

**Get Rid of Your "BUT!"**

**God Can Still Use You**
10. The story of Jonah can be found in the book of Jonah
11. Moses' story is found in Exodus 2:11-15
12. David is found in 2 Samuel 11 and 12
13. Rahab is found in Joshua 2 and 6:17
14. Mary Magdalene is found in Luke 8:2
15. Romans 8:38-39, NKJV
16. Genealogy that includes Rahab; Matthew 1:5

**Detour on the Road Trip**
17. Meyer, Joyce, *Do Yourself a Favor...Forgive*, Faithwords, 2012
18. James 5:13-15a, NKJV

**Sticks and Stones**

19. 1 Peter 5:6-7, Matthew 11:28-36, Jeremiah 33:3,
20. 2 Corinthians 5:17, NKJV

**Stop Listening to Lies**
21. James 4:7, NKJV
22. Isaiah 43:19, Amplified Bible
23. Romans 12:2, HCSB

**Deflating Balloons**
24. James 1:2-4, HCSB
25. Proverbs 25:21-22, NLT

**Past Is Past**
26. Psalm 103:12, 2 Corinthians 5:17-18, HCSB

**Take Off Your Mask**

**Finding Your Treasure**
27. Corinthians 4:7a, NLT
28. Psalm 103:6, Matthew 21:22, NKJV

**Do It Afraid**
29. Psalm 111:10, Hebrews 1:8, James 2:7, 1 Corinthians 14:33, NKJV

**Setting Boundaries**
30. Romans 16:17-18, Matthew 12:36-37, HCSB

**Shields Up!**
31. Ephesians 6:14-17, NKJV

**Mass Communicating**
32. WIBI Christian Radio station is now WBGL. You can listen to them online at www.wbgl.org.
33. The podcast to the radio show mentioned in the chapter is available at
    http://soundcloud.com/radiomelody/shelley-wilburn-podcast

**Healing Rain**
34. Psalm 25:1-7, NKJV

**Freedom**
35. 1 Peter 5:8-9, 10, NKJV
**Make Up Your Mind**
36. James 5:12, Isaiah 40:31, HCSB
**Moving Forward**
37. Colossians 4:2, HCSB
**Wisdom In Reconciling**
38. James 3:17, HCSB
39. James 1:5-6a, NKJV
**When Friendships Fail**
**Beauty for Ashes**
40. Isaiah 61:1-3a, 2 Chronicles 7:14, NKJV
41. Jeremiah 29:11-14a, NIV
**Water On the Rocks**
**Overcoming Fear**
42. *Underdog* cartoon; American animated television series debuted October, 3, 1964 on NBC network. Primarily sponsored by General Mills, Underdog continued in syndication until 1973. Ref. Wikipedia.
43. 2 Timothy 1:7, Romans 8:37, NKJV
**Label Makers**
44. Galatians 6:7-8, Isaiah 43:1b, NKJV
**Learning to Let Go**
45. Andy Stanley quote, *The Complete Guide to Christian Quotations*, Barbour Publishing, Inc., 2011, 170-47
**No One Like You**
46. Max Lucado quote, *The Complete Guide to Christian Quotations,* Barbour Publishing, Inc., 2011, 179-2
47. Romans 12:4, 6a, NKJV
**Cracked Pots**
48. 2 Corinthians 4:1-7, 8-9, NKJV

**Don't Miss the Point**
49. Proverbs 16:18, John 1:23, 26-27, Isaiah 40:3, NKJV
**From Duh to Aha!**
50. Psalm 139:23-24, NKJV
**Grace Who?**
51. Psalm 84:11, NKJV
Devotions mentioned can be seen at:
52. www.maxlucado.com
53. www.proverbs31.org
54. www.internetcafedevotions.com
55. www.joycemeyer.org
56. www.joelosteen.com
57. Lucado, Max, *Grace*, Thomas Nelson, 2012
58. Definition of Grace from www.dictionary.com
59. James 4:6, NKJV

**Do Yourself a Favor**
60. Psalm 103:12, 1 John 1:9, NKJV
61. Kay Arthur, Precept Ministries International, www.precept.org

**Got Junk in Your Trunk?**
62. 1 Peter 5:8, Philippians 4:8, Matthew 6:33, NLT

**Comfort Training**
63. Corinthians 1:4, NLT
64. Acts 1:8b, NIV

**Trust Issues**
65. Romans 8:28, John 8:44b, Psalm 56:3-4, HCSB

**Stepping Onto the Next Level**
66. Jeremiah 33:3, NKJV
67. John 10:10, NIV

**Perfectly, Powerfully, and Permanently**
68. Galatians 5:16-25, 22-23a, NLT

**Setbacks, Struggles, and Stress**
69. Peter 5:8, 1 John, 1:9, NKJV
70. Romans 16:20, NLT

**Moving On!**
71. John 14:6, NLT

**Can't Keep Me Down!**
72. Psalm 7:10, Psalm 39:7, Amplified Bible
73. Psalm 116:16, NKJV

**Where Do I Fit In?**

**Short-Circuited**
74. You can watch Creflo Dollar by visiting his website at www.creflodollarministries.org
75. 1 Peter 1:1b, NLV

**My Chains Are Gone!**
76. John 8:36, Proverbs 18:10, Psalm 61:3, Amplified Bible

**You Are On Purpose**
77. Isaiah 61:1-2, NLT
78. Luke 4:18-19, NLT

**Answer the Phone**
79. Jeremiah 1:5, 1 Corinthians 12:7-8, NLT

**Ch-Ch-Ch-Changes**
80. Hebrews 13:8, NLT
81. Jay Adams quote, *The Complete Guide to Christian Quotations*, 58-15
82. Philippians 3:21, NLT

**Leave Your Light On**
83. Matthew 5:14, 16b, James 4:7, NLT
84. Ephesians 6:13, NKJV

**Put Your Foot Down**
85. Ephesians 6:12, 6:14, Joshua 10:24b-25, NLT

**I Am a Lazarus**
86. John 11:4; 38-44, Jeremiah 29:11, Matthew 21:22,
87. John 11:25-26, HCSB
**A Year In My Life**
88. Luke 4:18-19, HCSB
**Stop People Pleasing**
89. Proverbs 17:1, NLT
90. Luke 1:46-47, 49, Amplified Bible
91. 1 Thessalonians 4:1a, NLT
**Because I Love You**
92. Ephesians 2:10, NLT
93. Reference to *Hotel California*, Eagles, 1977, Asylum Records
94. John 10:10; 8:36, NKJV
**Don't Back Up!**
95. Philippians 3:12, 13; Isaiah 43:2-3a, NLT
96. Hebrews 12:1b-2a, NKLV
**Grab a Hold**
97. Psalm 40:2-3; Luke 4:18-19, NLT
**Rose-Colored Glasses**
98. Ephesians 6:14; James 4:7-8a; John 8:36, NLT
**Zombies…The Walking Wounded**
99. Psalm 34:15, 17, NLT
100. Psalm 118:17, 147:3, Amplified Bible
101. 1 Peter 3:10-11, NLT
**What Are You Doing Here?**
102. The Story of Elijah is found in 1 Kings 19
103. 1 Kings 19:3a, 4; Psalm 139:1, 7; Isaiah 54:17, NLT
**Reckless**
104. Romans 8:31; Jeremiah 29:11, NLT

*105. Author's contacts can also be found in the Contacts section*

**Unlocking Your Door**

106. Shirer, Priscilla, *Gideon*, Lifeway Christian Resources, 2013

**God's Favor...Is NOW!**

107. Luke 4:18-19; Ephesians 2:10, NLT
108. Find Karla Akins at her website by going to www.karlaakins.com

**Far Out!**

109. Genesis 18:1-5; Judges 6:33-40; Luke 1:5-23; 1:26-38; 4:18-19, NLT

**Rescuing People**

110. Matthew 21:22, NKJV

**Discovering My More**

111. Jeremiah 32:27; Isaiah 54:17a, NKJV (paraphrased)

**Snakes in the Garden**

112. Story of Adam and Eve, Genesis, chapter 3
113. 2 Timothy 1:7, NLT

**Changing Your Life**

114. Proverbs 17:1; Psalm 138:8; Psalm 57:2-3, NLT

**Where Do I Go From Here?**

Three things to consider:
1) Is it positive?
2) Is it helpful?
3) Is it godly?

www.ingramcontent.com/pod-product-compliance
Lightning Source LLC
Chambersburg PA
CBHW050632300426
44112CB00012B/1758